# Alexan
# Father:

MW01008544

## his loves, and his death

**By Mark Steinberg**

# Table of Contents

# Alexander Hamilton: Founding Father

## Introduction

Much has been written about Alexander

Hamilton over the years. He has been the subject

of a musical and his life has been written about

in numerous books and articles. There is even an

organization based in New York City called the

Alexander Hamilton Awareness Society which

helps to perpetuate the ideas of Hamilton and

holds annual celebrations of his life on January

11, the date of his birth.  However, most

Americans know little about Hamilton. Indeed, it

is Washington, Jefferson and John Adams who

come to mind when people think of the

American Revolution and the founding of the

United States. Along with these great men, Hamilton made significant contributions to the development of the United States as we know it today and can be considered one of our country's most important founding fathers.

This book will give you an introduction to his life, his contributions, and the people who had an effect on his life at various stages. For you the reader, this book could be all you ever want to know about one of our founding fathers. For others, it could be a tantalizing introduction and spur you on to read more books about Hamilton or visit the sites in New York City where he lived and worked.

The book is divided into several chapters. Chapter I gives you a brief overview of his early life. Chapter II is about Hamilton's contributions during the American Revolution and his important relationship with George Washington. Chapter III is about Hamilton's career as statesman in the early days of the United States. It focuses on some of his major contributions that have had a lasting effect on the development of the country. Chapter IV is about Hamilton's family life and his affairs. Though he was a devoted husband to his wife Eliza, he also was a womanizer and his escapades did have an effect on his reputation. In Chapter V, the book focuses on what most Americans think of when they think of Hamilton, that is, the famous duel which he had with Aaron Burr. The duel ended his life at the age of 49. Finally, in the Epilogue, some concluding thoughts are offered. There is also a short bibliography which lists the sources used for this book. Some of the books are general biographies which others focus on particular aspects of Hamilton's life. I have also included some websites which might be of interest and urge you to visit the Grange if you come to New York to get some further insights into what made Hamilton tick.

## Chapter I – The Early Years

When Americans think of their founding fathers, they usually assume that they were born and brought up in one of the colonies that eventually became part of the United States of America. Washington, Jefferson, and Adams were in fact born in the colonies. However, Hamilton was born on January 11, 1755 outside of the United States on an island called Nevis, which is a British island in West Indies. His story, which begins on this island, is one of the great immigrant stories in American history. It is a so-called 'rags to riches' story about a young man born into poverty who immigrates to the United States, joins the aristocracy and becomes one of America's most important citizens.

Let us take a look at his childhood and early years. It was not an easy one. His maternal grandparents were John and Mary Faucette who had settled on Nevis. Nevis was the center of the sugar trade and the Faucettes owned a sugar plantation and several slaves. Seven children were born to the family; Hamilton's mother Rachel was the youngest.

The marriage however, was marred by the perpetual fighting between the parents and eventually, Mary Faucette decided to leave her husband and obtained a legal separation from him. She then took her youngest daughter Rachel and fled to St. Croix, another island in the West Indies not far from Nevis, where the two lived on the plantation of Mary's oldest daughter

Ann, who had married a prosperous landowner, James Lytton.

It was on St. Croix that Mary met a Danish man named Johann Lavien and married him. While he appeared to be a refined gentleman and the answer to Rachel's problems, Lavien was deep in debt. He had come to the island to make his fortune in the sugar trade but had not been successful. Far from being well settled and able to provide for Rachel, he had little to offer her once they were married. They did produce one son, Peter, but Rachel was treated very badly by Lavien and again decided to leave her husband for a better situation. This time however, there was no divorce and Lavien, enraged that Rachel would not only leave him but his toddler son, Peter, accused her of marital abandonment and adultery. The Danish court, which oversaw the legal aspects of St. Croix, agreed with Lavien and Rachel was thrown into prison.  She was released after several months and fled to the island of St. Kitts, another island in the West Indies.

Despite her prison time and the cruelty she suffered as Lavien's wife, Rachel was still an attractive woman and soon she met James Hamilton who had also come to the islands to make a fortune in the sugar trade. Hamilton was the son of a Scottish laird (lord) and was raised in a castle. His origins could be traced back to the so-called Cambuskeith line of Hamiltons who owned a family property known as the Grange castle. Hamilton had tried to be successful in the sugar trade but had largely failed.

Nevertheless, he must have appealed to Rachel and the two of them became involved. Wanting to start over, they left for Nevis where Rachel had grown up. However, they never married because Johann Lavien, her previous husband, who eventually divorced her, made sure that she was legally prohibited from ever marrying again. Thus the children that Rachel and James bore, James and Alexander, were considered bastards. Lavien called them 'whore-children'. Alexander's parentage would haunt him for the rest of his life and would be fodder for his enemies who felt that they could use it to slander him and demean him.

Back to our story. For all intents and purposes, Alexander and his brother James grew up in dire poverty on Nevis. James Hamilton tried to make things happen for his family but ultimately, he was unable to support them and left them in 1765 never to return.

Rachel, now left with two children, James, 12 and Alexander, 10, decided to move back to St. Croix, where she did manage to set up a fairly prosperous shop.  It was a kind of grocery store where she sold fish, flour, fruit and other goods. She and her boys lived upstairs in very Spartan quarters but she did obtain a set of 34 books for Alexander on a variety of topics.  This was the foundation of Alexander's education. These books, which included the poetry of Alexander Pope, Machiavelli's *The Prince*, and Plutarch's *Lives*, enabled young Hamilton to escape from his dreary existence and learn about other ways of life and ideas. Since he had no formal education as a young man, this set of books was a treasure trove for him and was extremely important in shaping the ideas which would propel him through American society and make him one of America's great leaders and thinkers.

Though Rachel tried to give her boys some semblance of a normal life, her efforts were cut short by tragedy. She and Alexander became ill with yellow fever and despite the efforts of local physicians, Rachel died on February 19, 1768. Alexander, who almost died, managed to recover from his illness. So at the age of twelve, Alexander Hamilton became an orphan. Though Rachel should have inherited something from Johann Lavien which she could have been passed onto her sons, the embittered and angry Lavien went to probate court and insisted that only his son Peter, the child Rachel had with him could inherit his estate. The courts sided with Lavien even though Peter Lavien was living comfortably in Beaufort, South Carolina and had not been in touch with his mother for eighteen years. Alexander and James were awarded nothing and were now orphaned and penniless.

The family that was left, namely Alexander's aunt Ann and her husband, James, decided that the solution for the two boys would be to appoint a guardian. James, their son became the two boys' guardian but he too sank into poverty and eventually committed suicide. Not a very good start for a young man. Here was Alexander penniless, orphaned at age twelve with no social connections to speak of and stuck on an island in the middle of the West Indies.

Yet all was not lost. His uncle, John Lytton took the boys in and helped them to get set up before he too died. Alexander's brother James was sent off to be an apprentice and Alexander got his first break. He was sent to work as a clerk for the New York trading house of Beekman and Cruger where he thrived. Though lacking in formal education, Alexander had already gotten a life education on the islands of Nevis and St. Croix. Indeed, from an early age he was very observant and carefully studied his surroundings.

For one thing, he noticed that even though Nevis was not a major world power, it occupied an interesting niche in the global trading economy for it exported a large amount of sugar to the rest of the world. Sugar became a sought after commodity. A second thing that Alexander noticed was that in order to keep the sugar export business going, thousands of slaves would arrive from Africa and be sent to work on the sugar plantations. This was the environment in which Alexander grew up. He was exposed to global trade at an early age and also witnessed the cruelty of the slave trade. Both of these experiences would influence him in later life and as a clerk for Beekman and Cruger, he was able to develop great skills as a manager and learn about the trading industry as an insider.

Alexander got another break when a prominent merchant on St. Croix, Thomas Stevens, offered to take the boy in and become his guardian. He introduced Alexander to a world he had never before known. Stevens was wealthy and provided the boy with a good life. So at this point, you are asking yourselves, why would a wealthy guy like Stevens take in an orphaned boy who was penniless? The answer is that it seems likely that Stevens was actually Alexander's true father. Stevens had a son Ned who bore a striking resemblance to Alexander and throughout the years, there has been a great deal of speculation on this topic. Perhaps he was the adulterer who Johann Lavien accused Rachel of seeing. It might also explain why Alexander and Ned became much closer than Alexander was with his brother James. In any case, Alexander lived with the Stevens family for many years.

Alexander Hamilton took up his new duties at Beekman and Cruger with a great deal of enthusiasm. As a clerk, he oversaw the imports and exports for the company. Indeed, the company supplied the island with everything it needed from timber to food and exported the island's goods to the international community. At the age of twelve, Hamilton was running the back office of a shipping company and as a result, learned the essential aspects of trade and commerce. At first, he worked for both owners but after a while, Beekman left the business and Cruger, who was ill, sailed for New York City.

With both bosses gone, Hamilton ended up running the entire business which included not only supervising the paperwork but also negotiating the contracts for exporting and importing, and determining the best shipping routes for the company ships to take. This was a great experience for Hamilton as he learned about every aspect of international trade and also about how to manage a company. Yet, despite this great opportunity, Hamilton was bored. He actually hated to be behind a desk and longed for another life. At one point, he wrote to his friend, Ned Stevens, who was already in New York attending college, that "I wish there was a war." Of course, there would be one which Hamilton would be heavily involved in but in the meantime, he was still stuck on that island and that was not his cup of tea.

Opportunity knocked in the form of a hurricane. A hurricane? Yes, a hurricane. The island of St. Croix was in the middle of the Caribbean Ocean and therefore it was very vulnerable to the many storms which roared across the ocean. One night, there was a ferocious storm on the island. Hurricane force winds battered the place and most people stayed indoors. Not Hamilton! He went outside and wrote down notes about the storm and then wrote a letter about the storm to a local newspaper, *The Royal Danish American Gazette.* The letter was full of incredible descriptions like 'The roaring of the sea and wind-fierce meteors flying about in the air....", and became an instant hit. Remember there was no such thing as social media in those days. Instead, newspapers were widely read and Hamilton's amazing letter got the attention it deserved. One man who saw the letter was Hugh Knox, a preacher who had been living in the Caribbean for several years. Knox had been sent by Aaron Burr's father, Reverend Aaron Burr Senior, to work as a priest in the islands. We will return to Burr in Chapter 5. Knox recognized

Hamilton's potential and together with a group of wealthy patrons, among them Cruger, raised enough money to send Hamilton to America to get an education.

The "hurricane letter" became Hamilton's ticket out of the West Indies. In October 1772, he boarded a ship for New York and never returned to his country of birth. Cruger, who was already in New York, had a large network in the business and academic worlds and through his connections, paved the way for Hamilton to go to college. When Hamilton arrived in New York, he was introduced to other people who would form his circle of friends and be influential in his life. Among them were William Livingston who would later become governor of New Jersey, Elias Boudinot, a trustee of the fledgling

Princeton University, and Aaron Burr, who would figure prominently in his later life.

Hamilton instantly took Burr as his model. Who wouldn't? The young man had entered Princeton at 13 and finished in two years. Hamilton wanted to do the same. But first, he attended Elizabethtown Academy in what is now Elizabeth, New Jersey to shore up his formal education since until then, he had essentially been self-educated. Armed with his newly acquired credential, Hamilton applied to Princeton and requested to have an accelerated program of study much like Burr. Much to Hamilton's disappointment, the president of Princeton, Reverend John Witherspoon, rejected Hamilton and suggested he apply elsewhere. Hamilton's other choice was King's College in

New York, which would later become Columbia University. Hamilton applied there and asked for the same accelerated program. This time he was accepted and allowed to pursue his studies in the way he had proposed.

At King's College, Hamilton dived into his studies and was a great student. He joined his friend Ned Stevens who remained his lifelong friend and compatriot. Along with being a great place to study, Hamilton learned about the first signs of the Revolutionary War. Already in his circle of friends there was talk of American resistance to Britain's rule. But King's College was a place where many of the students were loyal to the British. Hamilton at first was on the loyalist side and when talk of resisting the British came up, he often stood up for the monarchy leading some to call him a monarchist. In fact, though later he was to become a champion of the revolutionary cause, Hamilton 'sat on the fence' for a long time regarding which side he was on. Hamilton however, could not help but be interested in what he heard about the colonists who were agitating for liberty. New York was the center of the ferment and Hamilton, who had sat on the sidelines was gradually drawn into the circle of men who wrote, spoke and acted in defense of freedom from the British. Going forward, Hamilton would use his education and his flair for words to aid the cause. It would change his life.

As we look back on this first chapter of Hamilton's life, it is clear that Hamilton was destined for greatness. In spite of his early childhood years which were tragic, Hamilton was able to overcome these initial obstacles. Using whatever he had gleaned from his informal education, he was able to get the attention of powerful men through his writings and his ability to assume great responsibility at a very young age. Who would not be impressed with such a man? It is true he got some breaks from Cruger, Stevens, and Knox, but no one would have bet on him and raised money for him to go to America and get an education unless he was worthy of this investment.

Now that he was in America, he would thrive in a variety of ways. Just as in his early years, there were people with whom he had strong relationships that helped to shape his life. The next person to do this was George Washington.

That is the subject of the next chapter.

# Chapter II – Hamilton as Revolutionary

The first chapter of this book dealt with Hamilton's early years and his improbable journey from island poverty to a place at the table of wealth and position. This chapter describes his involvement in the American Revolution and his relationship with George Washington who became his mentor. As noted earlier, Hamilton was still a student at King's College when things began to heat up in the colonies. At first, he sided with the Tories (supporters of the British) but as events unfolded, his attitudes and ideas began to change. He was to become one of the biggest supporters of the Revolution and offered his brainpower and his abilities as a speaker and writer to the cause.

Of course, the event that got everyone going was the famous Boston Tea Party which took place on December 16, 1773. The British had imposed a variety of taxes on the colonists including a tax on legal documents, newspapers, sugar and tea in order to get revenue from the colonies. It was the tea tax which sent the colonists over the edge. Patriots in Boston, disguised as Indians, boarded British ships in Boston harbor and threw 342 crates of tea overboard with the local crowd cheering them on from the docks. The British retaliated by closing down Boston's port and imposing other "intolerable" penalties on the colonists.

It was the Tea Party event which proved to be the spark that ignited Hamilton's revolutionary ideals. No longer a monarchist, he gave a speech on the grounds of Princeton University suggesting that the destruction of the tea was necessary and that the colonists were properly asserting themselves and should boycott British goods. The speech was well received by those gathered at Princeton and marked Hamilton's first foray into the political maelstrom.

The colonists' cause continued to gain strength and became more organized. The First Continental Congress was convened. It was made up of representatives from almost all of the colonies and proclaimed a trade embargo on all British goods. This prompted reaction from those who were still sympathetic to the British cause. One such supporter was Samuel Seabury who wrote a series of pamphlets using the pen name *A Westchester Farmer* in which he denounced the whole revolutionary effort.

This was all Hamilton needed. He was itching for a fight and enjoyed taking on people whose positions he found distasteful. Seabury was a perfect target. In short order, Hamilton wrote his first political pamphlet called *A Full Vindication of the Measures of Congress* in which he supported the Continental Congress's right to boycott British goods. The pamphlet was eloquent, well argued, and established Hamilton as one of the foremost writers of his generation. No one else could have presented the arguments so well. Later, Seabury wrote a response to which Hamilton responded with an 80 page document ripping Seabury and his compatriots to shreds. Yes, people took notice of this young upstart who had the guts to go up against some of the most powerful people in the colonies.

The events leading up to full blown war continued to unfold in the colonies. The British government had declared that the rebels were a major threat and it was ready to put them down at any cost. On April 18, 1775, a large contingent of British soldiers marched out of Boston with the aim of capturing the ring leaders of the rebellion. When they reached Lexington and Concord, Massachusetts on April 19, they were met by a small group of rebels known as the Minutemen who fought back. Some of the Minutemen died but not before they had inflicted serious casualties on the British side. The colonists had shown the British they meant business and fired off the famous 'shots that were heard around the world.'

The War was on and Hamilton who heard about the battle at Lexington and Concord saw his chance. He immediately joined the New York State militia company where he distinguished himself as a soldier. Not content just to march with his compatriots, he taught himself the rules of military warfare, the operation of guns and became knowledgeable about military strategies and tactics. Much like his early self-education, this newly acquired knowledge would prove invaluable to him and distinguish him from others who were part of the War effort.

At this point in the story, it is worthwhile to leave Hamilton at his post with the New York militia and focus on his future mentor George

Washington. Washington came to be an important leader in the Revolutionary War in a different way than Hamilton. While Hamilton was flexing his muscles as a writer and arguing against the taxes imposed on the colonists by the British, Washington, a wealthy landowner, was living in Virginia. He was an influential man in Virginia and a member of Virginia's House of Burgesses which was one of the governing bodies of the State. He was also a war hero having distinguished himself as a military leader in the recent French and Indian War. Washington heard about the taxes, especially the Stamp Tax Act which taxed documents and newspapers. He immediately took a stand against the Stamp Act and with his fellow legislators, voted in favor of supporting the boycott of British goods in

Virginia. Washington foresaw that the trouble between the British government and the American government could erupt into full scale war. He wrote several letters about this in which he outlined the grievances of the colonists. Despite his support for the colonists, he still hoped that the British would find a way to work out the issues with the colonists.

Along with six other members of the Virginia legislature, Washington was elected as a delegate to the First Continental Congress that was to be held in Philadelphia. Part of the reason he was elected was because the delegates felt that if there was to be a full blown war, Washington could successfully command an army. They knew this because several years before the Revolutionary War, Washington had distinguished himself in the French and Indian War as a warrior and leader.  Washington and his fellow delegates joined the delegates from the other colonies and worked on a Declaration of Rights and Grievances and other measures that they hoped would be accepted by the British. But there was to be no reconciliation. After the battle of Lexington and Concord, the colonists were energized and prepared for war. Washington was selected to be commander-in-chief and marched into New York City. Hamilton stood in the crowd and watched the new commander-in-chief.

But there was very little time for celebrating as the British were ready to attack the colonists and clearly had more firepower and troops at their disposal. They sailed into New York harbor with a vast armada of ships on July 2, 1776. Two days later, the colonists published the Declaration of Independence making it clear that there was no turning back. Washington gathered his troops in New York and tried desperately to stave off the British advance. Among the troops was Alexander Hamilton, the newly minted Captain of the first battalion, Fifth artillery unit. Washington retreated from New York and lost many men. During the retreat, Hamilton commanded his troops with great skill which did not go unnoticed by Washington and his officers. Washington who witnessed Hamilton's exploits is said to have been charmed by Hamilton and in admiration of his great skill as a military man.

Washington was forced to retreat and Hamilton and his artillery troops provided the needed cover for Washington's troops to get to safer ground. Finally, on December 26, Hamilton and his unit helped Washington catch the British by surprise near Trenton. It was a victory savored by the colonists and Hamilton had played a large role in securing it.

Despite this victory at Trenton, the British were not through. In early January, General Cornwallis, who commanded a large number of British troops, decided to attack the colonial army near Princeton. Washington and his army used the tactic of surprise and instead of meeting Cornwallis and his men on the battlefield where they were expected, Washington led his men in a round-about way to the rear of the college at Princeton. Cornwallis was not prepared and Washington was successful in his strategy. As his men proceeded to round up prisoners, the legend goes that Hamilton set up his cannon in the courtyard of the college and sent a cannonball through the brick building which shattered the portrait of King George II in the chapel. Whether this happened or not, the British soldiers who were in the chapel surrendered.

The battles of Trenton and Princeton were important for two reasons. One of them was that with the dual victories, Washington's troops who had been demoralized because of so many defeats, revived and a new spirit spread throughout the army. The other important reason related to Hamilton. Throughout these battles, the young leader had distinguished himself and people began to notice this. He had a certain air about him and had managed to put together a disciplined group of men who stood out among the troops. Hamilton had made a name for himself and from that moment on, his life would never be the same.

After the victory at Trenton, Washington set up his headquarters in Morristown, New Jersey. Hamilton was exhausted and retreated with his troops to Bucks County, Pennsylvania, across the river from Washington. Hamilton was lying in his bed recuperating and gathering his strength for another round of battles when he received a note from General Washington on January 20, 1777 inviting him to become his aide-de-camp. Hamilton was not happy about this turn of events. True, the position of aide-de-camp came with an appointment to lieutenant colonel and he would be part of Washington's coveted inner circle. But Hamilton wanted glory. He wanted to be in the thick of battle not behind a desk. He dreaded that it would be a repeat of his days working for Cruger and Beekman in St. Croix.

Yet Hamilton could not say no. So, he got up from his sickbed and traveled to Morristown to accept Washington's invitation. On March 1, 1777, Hamilton was officially appointed as Washington's aide-de-camp. This was the beginning of a relationship that would at times be stormy and at other times, be wonderful. Hamilton was not the easiest person to get along with and nor was Washington. But Washington needed Hamilton desperately. He needed someone that he could delegate administrative tasks to so that he could concentrate on strategies for beating the British. The army was in need of someone who could organize its supplies and men. Finally, he knew that Hamilton could write and think deeply and more than anything, he needed someone who could articulate his ideas and present them well to his staff, the army and the rest of the colonists. Hamilton was the man for all these tasks.

For his part, Hamilton discovered that Washington was extremely demanding, perhaps more than any other boss he had worked for. Washington expected his staff to be on call day and night and to carry out his wishes. He was open to suggestions but ultimately was the commander-in-chief and made the final call. Washington did reward his staff and valued ability and brains rather than the pedigree of aristocratic birth. Though Washington came from aristocracy, he created a meritocracy in his army amongst his staff, which enabled everyone who had talent to advance. Hamilton, who was extremely bright and talented suddenly had a vehicle for advancing upward through the ranks.

The relationship between Hamilton and Washington blossomed; he and the General became indispensable to one another. Washington increasingly relied on Hamilton and trusted him with everything. Hamilton wrote the bulk of Washington's letters and after a while, he signed Washington's name to them. Together with the rest of the staff, Hamilton worked around the clock to help Washington with the war effort. This included strategizing about upcoming battles and determining the course of the war which would ultimately affect the men who were under Washington's command.

After resting and regrouping in Morristown, Washington and Hamilton who had a shared vision of the War, and believed wholeheartedly in the cause of the colonists, resumed their battles with the British. Alas, they were unsuccessful. No matter what the Continental army tried, the British were there to outsmart them and outman them. After leaving New York, the British under General Howe went south with 18,000 men and proceeded to decimate the Continental army in and around Philadelphia. It was time for action on the American side and Washington called upon his most trusted aid, Hamilton, to carry out his orders and try to turn the tide which seemed to be continually against the rebel army. He dispatched Hamilton along with General Henry "Light-Horse Harry" Lee to burn the flour mills along the Schuylkill River near Philadelphia in order to deprive the British soldiers of supplies.  Hamilton accomplished the task he was assigned but lost many men and barely escaped with his life. He then was sent to Philadelphia to warn the people about the advancing British army. His other mission in Philadelphia was to commandeer as many supplies as possible from the citizens of the city so as to deprive the British again of securing precious supplies which they needed for the troops. This too, was accomplished.

In another indication of Washington's trust in Hamilton, he sent Hamilton in November 1777 to meet with General Horatio Gates, who had not performed well during the War, to surrender a large number of troops which were under his command. Gates was furious but Hamilton continued to press him until he surrendered the troops. Washington wrote to Hamilton that he approved of everything he had done.

Before going on with the story of the War, we will pause briefly to get some further insight into the relationship between Hamilton and Washington. This is most important because it provides a backdrop for the War effort. Hamilton and Washington saw eye to eye on most issues but there were some where Hamilton and Washington had very different points of view. Also, the upbringing of the two men which was vastly different played a part in shaping their relationship and their views.

Though Hamilton and Washington saw eye to eye on lots of issues, they did have significant differences of opinion on the issue of slavery and the inclusion of freed black men in the continental army. Washington was a wealthy landowner from the South who owned slaves and was very conflicted about the role of slaves in the Revolutionary War. He and his officers had received requests from black men to participate in the war effort. Initially, Washington rejected these requests. However, after thinking it through, he decided to let free black men enlist in the army. While freed black men could enlist, Washington was against allowing slaves to do the same. Arming slaves he believed, was the first step in encouraging them to seek freedom from their masters. Since slaves were an important part of the economic engine of the South, Washington had no choice but to side with his wealthy landowner friends who were slave owners

On the other hand, Hamilton had witnessed first-hand the cruelty that the slaves on St. Croix and Nevis suffered at the hands of their masters, and was of the opposite mind when it came to the issue of slavery. He thought the system of slavery, so widely practiced in the South, was degrading and demeaning. He believed that slaves should be allowed to arm themselves as a first step toward their freedom and urged the leaders of the Continental Congress to allow slaves to enlist and bear arms. Washington remained firmly against this action and believed that it would only stir up trouble and prove to be distracting to the American war effort. In the end, the Congress did pass a resolution enabling the slaves to enlist. As Washington predicted, the landowners in the Southern colonies such as South Carolina and Georgia were outraged and became disenchanted to a certain extent about the war effort.

This difference of opinion between Washington and Hamilton revealed that they viewed some issues from very different perspectives. In some way, it is easy to understand why each man thought the way he did; it was to a great extent based on their respective backgrounds. Washington relied on slaves to run his plantation and viewed this two-tiered system of slaves and masters as an integral part of the culture in which he lived. On the other hand, Hamilton was more idealistic and did not want to perpetuate the horrors he had witnessed as a young man. At a later stage in their relationship, both men would come closer to agreeing on this issue of slavery rather than disagreeing on it.

Another incident that took place during the war which also pointed out how different these two men were. This was the infamous incident in which one of Washington's most trusted men, General Benedict Arnold, turned traitor to the colonial cause. General Arnold, who had distinguished himself in some of the Revolutionary War battles, was put in charge of West Point, a military base and strategic point on the Hudson River. In September 1780, Washington, accompanied by Hamilton and some other officers, went to West Point to inspect the fort. They had planned to meet with Arnold. However, when Washington arrived,

Arnold was not there. Instead, he was taking part in a plot to have Washington captured and deliver West Point to the enemy. Arnold had deliberately not maintained the West Point position so that the British would be able to easily capture it.

While Washington and his staff were waiting for Arnold, a messenger arrived stating that a British officer named Major Andre, who was dressed in civilian clothes, had been captured with a map and other plans regarding West Point. When Arnold realized that Andre had been captured, he fled from his home and boarded a British boat that was moored downstream on the Hudson. Washington meanwhile realized what had happened and sent Hamilton and his men after Arnold. But it was too late. Arnold was gone.

Washington turned to his aides and said, "Arnold has betrayed us. Whom can we trust now?" He and Hamilton then went back to Arnold's house and found Mrs. Arnold, who was hysterical and holding her baby. Hamilton and Washington tried their best to comfort Mrs. Arnold not knowing that she was putting on an act so that Arnold would have enough time to escape. Both men were completely disgusted by what happened that day.

After his capture, Major Andre was taken to Tappan, New York, tried and convicted. Washington ordered that he be hanged. Hamilton, who had spent some time with the prisoner, pleaded with Washington to have Andre shot to preserve his honor. Hamilton thought that Andre was a very refined man and a gentleman and that he did not deserve to be hanged like a common criminal. Despite Hamilton's pleas, Andre was indeed hung.

This incident also sheds some light on the characters of the two men. Both of them lived by a gentleman's code of honor. Hamilton however was ready to defend this code of honor at any cost. He viewed Washington's refusal to grant Andre an honorable death as a betrayal of the code. This loyalty to the code of honor would ultimately lead to his famous duel with Aaron Burr which is the subject of Chapter V. Washington, though a gentleman and someone who respected the code was more inclined to see beyond it and look at the bigger picture. For him, hanging Andre sent a message to his troops and the rest of the world that he would act in a fair manner on such delicate matters and that in doing so, could not be criticized for bypassing the principles by which he commanded the army and lived his life.

In the middle of all this turmoil, Hamilton became engaged to Eliza Schuyler, the daughter of Phillip Schuyler, one of the wealthiest men in New York. The two fell madly in love and got married. We will return to Eliza and Alexander and their marriage in a later chapter (Chapter IV). It is just important to know that this very involved military man was also a devoted lover and family man.

The issue of honor and how each man approached it did continue to influence their relationship with one another. In early 1781, Hamilton and Washington had a disagreement that had a far reaching effect on their relationship. At this point in the War, Washington was thoroughly exhausted and though he had achieved some victories, had to deal with men who were discouraged and rebellious because they had not been in paid in quite a while. The War was far from over and he probably did not see victory in sight.

One evening, Hamilton was at Washington's headquarters and was going down the stairs while Washington stood at the top of the stairs. Washington asked to speak to Hamilton and Hamilton told him that he would be right back after he delivered an important letter. He then continued on his way and was detained by a conversation with his friend, the Marquis de Lafayette, a Frenchman who was helping out with the war effort. Hamilton then hurried back to Washington only to be confronted by the General who started to yell at him for keeping him waiting. Washington laid into him and told him that Hamilton had treated him with disrespect. Hamilton was taken aback by Washington's behavior. Instead of taking a few breaths and composing himself, Hamilton replied that he was not aware that he had treated the General with disrespect. Hamilton sometimes led his pride get the better of him and in this instance, it did. Turning on his heel, Hamilton told the General that "since you have thought it necessary to tell me, so we part". Washington said something to the effect that if Hamilton wanted it that way, that was fine with him. And so the two parted ways in a very abrupt manner.

After an hour, Washington sent Hamilton an apology for his behavior. He offered to meet with Hamilton privately and expressed his regret at his outburst. However, Hamilton was not interested in accepting the apology. He was also counseled by his friend Lafayette and his wife Eliza to patch things up. Hamilton, who had a stubborn streak and some say, an exaggerated need to adhere to a strict code of honor. Hamilton's actions were perhaps just his excuse for getting out from under Washington's thumb. He told everyone that he disliked being Washington's "boy" as he was sometimes called and that he only accepted the position of aide-de-camp because he wanted to help the cause of the Revolutionary War.  Being Washington's right hand man seemed to him to be a good way of doing that. In the interests of the war effort, Hamilton agreed not to discuss what had happened between him and Washington. However, he remained deeply hurt about the incident.

Washington and Hamilton were to meet again at the Battle of Yorktown but their relationship was never the same after the rift on the stairs. Was this incident an example of a young man who did not know how to control his temper? Did he act in a rash manner or was he justified? Everyone has an opinion on what happened.  While Hamilton may have regretted his very impetuous actions towards Washington, he never made an effort to re-establish the close personal relationship he had had with the General. He did write some formal letters to Washington but none that indicated he had ever been part of Washington's inner circle. Instead, he began to think about the next steps in his career. He was now free from his "desk job" and the War was still going on.

Washington meanwhile was regrouping and getting ready for his next battles with the British. His chief adversary, General Cornwallis was also preparing for a fight. Hamilton was itching for a command and wrote to Washington requesting one. Washington was angry and wrote back to Hamilton that he was embarrassed by Hamilton's request and that he would not be pressured into giving him a command. There were other men ahead of him. Yet, Washington finally relented and gave him the command of a light infantry unit. Hamilton was happy about this but didn't know if he would ever see the action he craved.

Since the British had fortified New York to the hilt, it appeared to be an impossible target. So Washington decided on another strategy. He knew that Cornwallis had taken his army to Yorktown, Virginia and was engaged in fortifying the area. Washington planned to attack Cornwallis in Virginia and marched there with his men. In order to have enough strength and fire power, he joined forced with the French. In a bold move, he also made fake preparations to attack New York where Sir Henry Clinton, a British general was stationed. Clinton was tricked into believing that he was going to be attacked and so instead of joining Cornwallis, he remained with his troops in New York. This left Cornwallis vulnerable which was just what Washington wanted.

In late September 1781, Washington sent Hamilton to Yorktown with his other troops to attack the city. Cornwallis saw that he was being attacked and dug in as best he could. He built twenty foot high earthen works from which the British soldiers could easily pick off the advancing soldiers. However, the Americans did not give up and eventually they forced Cornwallis to retreat to an underground cave. The British forces were depleted and vulnerable.

There was one more assault left which would finish off the job. At first, Washington appointed Lafayette to take charge. Hamilton wanted to command the final assault and finally Washington relented and gave him the go-ahead. On October 14, Hamilton and his men charged the earthen works where the British were holding on. Hamilton then joined forces with the French army, and together, they bombarded the British positions. Cornwallis attempted to escape but was prevented from doing so by bad weather.

It was all over. On October 19, 1781, Cornwallis surrendered. In a show of personal pride, Cornwallis sent his underling Brigadier General Charles O'Hara to present his sword to Washington. Washington refused to accept it and instead sent General Benjamin Lincoln, who earlier in the War with his brigade of black soldiers, had fought against the British in Charleston, South Carolina. This was a curious move for Washington since he was the commanding general, but many believe that he did this to show his appreciation to the black men who had fought so valiantly in the War.

Whatever the case, the Continental army took approximately 8000 British prisoners that day. It would take another two days before the War finally concluded with a cease fire. Two years later, in 1783, the Treaty of Paris was signed and the Revolutionary War was officially over. On November 25 of that year, the British finally sailed out of New York Harbor. The Americans lowered the Union Jack which was the British flag and replaced it with their own. They were free of the British.

Our hero, Alexander Hamilton, had fought valiantly during the War and earned the admiration of everyone. What would happen now? After Yorktown, Hamilton went home to his wife Eliza.  In March, Hamilton resigned from the army and never returned to active service. He lived in Albany, New York with his growing family and studied law. He thought that he would settle down and leave government forever. Hamilton passed the New York State Bar after six months of study. Would Hamilton remain on the sidelines? Hardly likely.

Hamilton had already been thinking about how to organize the American government once the War was over. He had expressed many of his views to members of Congress and other powerful and influential people. His main idea was that there should be a strong central government which would govern the States. His reasoning in part came from watching what happened during the Revolutionary War when the army badly needed funding. Both he and Washington saw how the States were often downright defiant about providing funding for the war effort. They often hoarded money and supplies so that if the British attacked their territory, they could retaliate. This tactic often proved disastrous as the army needed supplies and there was no other way to raise money in order to buy them.  Also, some of the States sometimes failed to send the required number of delegates to the Continental Congress so that it was frequently difficult to get the quorum needed to administer the War. Hamilton believed that the only way the new country was going to succeed was to take the power away from the States and put it in the hands of a strong Congress and a strong Executive branch. Otherwise, the decentralized government would lead to the collapse of the army and ultimately whatever gains the colonists had made in securing their freedom from Britain, would be lost.

Along with a weak government that deferred most of the time to State rule, the country had an inadequate financial infrastructure. While Hamilton was still in the Army, he was nominated for the post of superintendent of finance which was a post created by the Continental Congress to oversee the financial affairs of the colonists. The Congress had begun to see that the States were doing a very bad job of managing their money and this post was their answer to the fiscal crisis which they feared could sink the whole country. Washington was consulted on the nomination and said that even though he did not know if Hamilton was knowledgeable about finances, he had a great deal of general knowledge and Washington thought he could be successful in this role.

Despite this great endorsement, Hamilton was passed over in favor of Robert Morris who was very wealthy and who had provided monies to the colonists by drawing on his own private credit. Hamilton, though disappointed, decided to get involved in the discussion. He proceeded to write a thirty-one page pamphlet on the need to create a central bank and develop a credit system for the Revolution and ultimately the new country if the colonists were successful in their war effort. He forecast an enormous budget deficit for that time - four to five million dollars – and suggested ways to deal with this issue. He also advocated imitating the British system of borrowing by setting up a national debt. He wrote that if a national debt was not excessive it would be a blessing and help the Union.

Morris liked what he read and wrote back that he was already starting to set up the infrastructure for a Bank of North America. As a result of this exchange, Morris and Hamilton became friends and remained in touch regarding the financial needs of the country. In fact, it was Morris who got Hamilton to leave the quiet civilian life of being a lawyer and family man. In May 1782, Morris asked Hamilton to become the tax receiver for the State of New York. Hamilton was only twenty-seven years old but he accepted the job. This proved momentous for his career as his appointment as receiver involved interacting with the state legislators who liked him. They eventually appointed him to the New York delegation to the Continental Congress that would be meeting in Philadelphia in November.

With the War officially over in 1783, the men who had served the country so well and achieved victory began returning home. Many of them had not been paid in many years for their efforts and demanded back pay. Hamilton persuaded Washington to meet with them. After Washington admitted that he was gray and nearly blind as a result of devoting himself to the country, the rebellious soldiers backed down. However, it became increasingly clear that something had to be done to pay these men who had served the cause.

In December, 1783, Hamilton moved his family from Albany to 57 Wall Street. There he developed a successful law practice. To many people's dismay, Hamilton frequently took on unpopular defendants. In one case, he defended the loyalists who had gone off to England and left their property. These people now returned and demanded to occupy their homes and restitution for the damage that occurred to their properties. Hamilton wanted justice to be done and defended these people despite being criticized for it. Many people were shocked that Hamilton would support these people and accused him of being a traitor. But he thought that that if the Tories were driven out, it would backfire on merchants and traders who depended on the Tory business for their livelihood.

One famous trial that Hamilton participated involved in concerned a widow named Elizabeth Rutgers who had left New York when the British occupied it. She abandoned her property which included a brewery in 1776 and two years later, two people, Benjamin Waddington and Evelyn Pierrepont took over the brewery. Mrs. Rutgers filed a suit against these people and Hamilton chose to defend her. He questioned the legality of the Trespass Act which she was using for her defense. Hamilton asserted that in renting Mrs. Rutger's property to Waddington, the British had done nothing wrong and that New York's Trespass Act was a violation of the Treaty which had been signed between the British and Americans at the end of the War.

By encouraging the court to review this law, Hamilton again contributed to the development of the country. He asked the court to conduct a judicial review of the law. This was unprecedented in the courts of the new country. Judicial review which is now a part of our legal system, allows the courts to review a law and declare it illegal if necessary. He finally negotiated a settlement with Mrs. Rutgers; it was a great triumph for Hamilton. Not only had he secured a victory for his Tory client; he had also contributed to the development of the legal system.

It had been an amazing journey so far. Hamilton had risen from nowhere to become a trusted member of Washington's inner circle. He had distinguished himself as a soldier, a leader, and a thinker. He was already engaged in developing the basic outline for the federal government and other institutions that would be the foundation for the future United States of America. He had married into a wealthy family and became an aristocrat seemingly overnight. In the next chapter, we will look more closely at some of his accomplishments as a statesman and leader in the new country which had emerged following the end of the Revolutionary War.

## CHAPTER III – HAMILTON AS STATESMAN

Hamilton was now tax receiver of New York State and living in New York City with his family. Hamilton was on his way to becoming a statesman in the new country that was just being formed. In this chapter, we will look at some of his accomplishments as a statesman in the areas of banking, structuring of the federal government as we know it today, and manufacturing. We will also look at his relationship with one of the other founding fathers, Thomas Jefferson, who had very different views about how the country should be set up.

We will start with the Articles of Confederation which constituted an agreement between the original 13 states in the United States. It served as the first constitution of the country. The Articles, which were not ratified by the States until 1781, provided a way for the Continental Congress to conduct the American Revolution and deal with other issues that arose during the early days of the Republic.   Hamilton and other colonial leaders were not happy with the Articles. There were no formal structures for governing or banking. As described in the previous chapter, the States had a lot of power and were often not very willing to contribute the money they had to the general government coffers.

Indeed, the central government had no way to tax the States.  After the Revolutionary War, the country was in effect bankrupt because both the federal and state governments had no way to deal with the enormous debt that had been incurred as result of the War. Not only that. Throughout the colonies, many people were also mired in debt. Farmers were struggling to pay their taxes and other debts. There was a lot of unrest in the colonies as Hamilton feared.

In 1783, while he was tax receiver for New York, Hamilton proposed that a convention be held of all the States in order to give the Congress complete power over matters such as finance, trade, foreign affairs, war and peace. In effect, he was advocating for a convention to revise the Articles of Confederation. However, he never got the support for the convention. Instead, in 1785, James Madison of Virginia and a powerful man in Congress called for a convention to discuss the trade issues that were confronting America. Hamilton was chosen as a delegate to the convention which was called The Annapolis Convention. Hamilton and the other delegates were given the job of figuring out how to set up a system for regulating trade among the States. The document which was produced called for a more centralized federal government which would have power to regulate trade and other matters related to the newly formed Union. The report produced at the Annapolis Convention was a first step toward a stronger document but it would not go anywhere until an event occurred that stirred everyone in the Congress to finally act.

The event was the rebellion of debt-ridden farmers in Massachusetts. These farmers, many of whom had fought in the Revolution, were disgusted. They were deep in debt because paper money was worthless, and they could not pay the merchants and shopkeepers who were demanding that they pay up their debts. Many of these farmers lost their homes and were thrown into prison.  Finally, they banded together to make demands and sent petitions to the Massachusetts General Court asking for relief from their taxes, and for help in saving their properties.  When their demands were not met, using the only weapons they had – pitchforks and other farm tools– they shut down courthouses and in late September, a large contingent of farmers blocked the ability of the

Massachusetts Supreme Court to convene for sessions.

 The rebellion was led by a man named Daniel Shays, who had been a captain in the colonial militia. He organized the farmers who put on their old Continental Army uniforms and marched through the countryside determined to have their demands met. It was War again but this time it was a Civil War. Shays and his 'army' said they were out to overthrow the government of the State of Massachusetts and that they would stop at nothing to get what they wanted. In late January 1787, more than 2000 rebels under the leadership of Shays attacked the federal arsenal in Springfield, Massachusetts. They were met by a large contingent of militiamen who won the skirmish. The rebellion was over and though the Massachusetts courts wanted to punish the rebels, they were ultimately pardoned by the Governor of the State.

While this rebellion did not play out on the national stage, it was a major catalyst for change. Many of the leaders of the country were shocked at what had occurred. Washington was appalled. He had just spent eight years fighting the British so that everyone in the country could be free and now he feared that his efforts were going to be for nothing. Many Americans were now concerned that the confederation of states was very fragile and would not survive. Hamilton was silent in the face of the rebellion and its aftermath because he sympathized with the rebels and knew that a solution had to be found. Indeed, there were major economic issues which needed to be addressed if the country was going to thrive. He warned that if nothing was done to unite the States under a strong federal government, the States would fight amongst themselves.

Finally, it became clear that the Articles of Confederation had to be revised. Hamilton became a delegate to the Convention and in May 1787, the delegates assembled to figure out how to strengthen the Articles. This historic meeting turned into the Constitutional Convention which produced the Constitution of the United States. This meeting was momentous because the Constitution became the basis for how the government of the United States would be structured. It is hard to believe that if this document had not been created, Americans would have a very different way of life. Hamilton played a big part in the development of the Constitution. During this time, he renewed his relationship with George Washington who became the President of the Convention and its leader.

Hamilton and his fellow delegates began to deliberate about the different aspects of the Constitution. There were various opinions on how to set up the government. One plan, which was suggested by Edmund Randolph, a delegate from Virginia. The plan, known as the Virginia Plan, called for dividing the government into three branches: the legislative branch which would be divided into two houses and have representatives in each house based on a state's population; the executive branch; and the judicial branch, which would oversee all of the laws of the Land. Randolph was not in favor of one person being in charge of the executive branch because to him, it was just like having a king. Another delegate, William Paterson, offered the New Jersey Plan, which essentially just strengthened the Articles of Confederation but did not include having a strong national government. The delegates continued to debate amongst themselves but were essentially at an impasse. They could not agree on anything.

Hamilton, who had voted for the Virginia Plan, finally decided to state what he believed. He went before the delegates and suggested his own plan. His plan called for a senate which took as its model, the House of Lords in Britain, in which members were elected for life and a monarch, who would also be elected for life. He stated that because these elected officials would be in office for life, they would not be tempted to engage in corrupt behavior such as taking bribes from their constituents. A key part of the plan was a system of checks and balances which the branches of government would be able to use so as to prevent one branch from becoming too powerful. The plan seemed to be based on the government from which the colonialists had just liberated themselves. What was he thinking? Hamilton just wanted a strong government with a strong leader and an elected body of officials who could govern well. He was afraid that the country would never be united and that it would revert back to a government run by the States each with its own agenda. The delegates listened politely to Hamilton's ideas but did not readily accept them. Many did not like the idea that the elected officials would be lifetime positions. They also labeled Hamilton a monarchist, which Hamilton did not like.

Hamilton raised another key point which reflected his origins as an immigrant. The other plans that had been suggested by the delegates called for members of Congress and other elected officials to be born in the United States. They would also need to live in the United States for a certain period of time in order to run for office. Hamilton objected to this obviously because he himself had been born outside of the United States. It was interesting that despite the fact that Hamilton was playing such a large role in the creation of the document we now call the

Constitution, he still had to deal with the fact that he was an 'outsider' and not a native born son.

In any case, the debate continued and became deadlocked. Hamilton along with many of his fellow delegates, left the convention and returned home. The other delegates from New York left and never returned so there ended up being no official New York delegation.

During this period, an interesting thing happened. Hamilton and Washington began to exchange letters on the state of affairs in the country. Washington was very upset at the deadlock that he had just witnessed and Hamilton too wrote of his fear that the convention might fail. The letters served as a way for Hamilton and Washington to renew their friendship. In fact, Washington at one point wrote that he missed Hamilton and wished that he had not gone back to New York. Clearly, Washington needed his company and looked forward to once again working with Hamilton. He had never doubted Hamilton's ideas and now needed Hamilton's brainpower and persuasive abilities to get the country going.

Finally, after much deliberation, a compromise was reached by the delegates. For the legislative branch, there would be two houses. The Senate would be made up of two senators from each state and the House of Representatives would be made up of representatives from each State with the number reflecting how many people lived in the state. The President would be elected for a four year term and be eligible for re-election.

Other points were ironed out and on September 17, 1787, Hamilton and others signed the document. Hamilton's signature did not count because there was no official New York delegation. Nevertheless, his signature was there.

Hamilton left the Convention with mixed feelings. He thought that the document which had been produced was flawed. But he was committed to getting it ratified especially in his own State of New York. He began to think of ways in which he could persuade the members of New York's government and other government officials in the various States to adopt the document they had all worked so hard to create. The result was a series of essays known as *The Federalist Papers*. We will turn to them next because they were so important in getting the Constitution ratified and also because this series of essays showed off Hamilton's ability to write and persuade.

*The Federalist Papers* are one of Hamilton's most enduring contributions. Hamilton wrote a series of essays designed to lay out the case for ratifying the Constitution. This was not an easy task. There were a lot people who were Anti-Federalists, that is, they opposed the Constitution and everything it stood for. A few months after the Constitutional Convention, James Madison, who was Hamilton's ally at the time, informed Washington, that there was trouble ahead regarding ratification. Hamilton took it upon himself to be the chief spokesperson for the ratification effort. In those days, there was no technology to get the word out. But there were print newspapers which were the way most people got their ideas out to large numbers of people. Hamilton's idea was to publish a series of essays which would outline the need for a Constitution. He wrote many of them himself and eventually got help from James Madison and another friend, John Jay. There were 85 essays in all. Hamilton wrote 51 of them, Madison wrote 29 and Jay wrote 5.

Hamilton wrote his essays under the pseudonym 'Publius'. The first essay appeared on October 27, 1787, in *The New York Independent Journal*. Hamilton argued that Americans were facing an extremely important decision about the future of their country. They could go the way of the Anti-Federalists who were against big government and advocated for States to govern themselves or they could ratify the Constitution and set up a centralized structure that would enable the country to thrive and grow. Hamilton also argued for a strong executive branch as well as an independent judicial branch of government.

Nine states were needed to ratify and one by one they voted to ratify the Constitution. However, in New York, Hamilton faced significant challenges with respect to ratification. The Governor of the State, Governor Clinton was opposed to ratification and marshalled his forces to fight Hamilton. It was the fight of his life even though the Constitution was already law. After much wrangling back and forth, Hamilton succeeded in persuading his fellow New Yorkers to vote in favor. On July 26, 1788, New York State joined the other States in ratifying this important document. Great celebrations followed. Hamilton and his compatriots had achieved a great victory. And just as important, Washington and Hamilton were once more together and ready to build a nation. The next part of our story deals with Hamilton's time as a member of Washington's cabinet.

George Washington was elected president of the newly formed Union on February 4, 1789. Washington initially tapped Robert Morris to be his Secretary of the Treasury. However, Morris declined and suggested that Washington appoint Hamilton. Washington had not thought of Hamilton as a choice for the Treasury slot. He had a high opinion of him but did not know that whether he was sufficiently knowledgeable about finance.  He also thought Hamilton was too young to assume this important position. Finally, he agreed to appoint Hamilton, and on September 11, 1789, Hamilton became the nation's first Secretary of the Treasury.

Contrary to Washington's view, Hamilton was no stranger to banking. In fact, as we noted in Chapter II, he had been involved in the area of finance during the Revolutionary War. After being passed over for Superintendent of Finance for the Continental Congress, he did as you recall, write a very long paper about the need for a central bank. Also, he did have experience in his home state of New York. He had been the tax receiver of the State and he had been instrumental in founding the Bank of New York in New York City. This was New York's first financial institution and it became the cornerstone of New York's ascendancy as a financial powerhouse. In 1784, when the Bank was chartered, Hamilton had already realized that the financial health of the colonies after the Revolutionary War was poor. Many people did not understand the purpose of a bank and so Hamilton had an uphill battle to get the Charter approved by the Governor of New York. It finally opened as a private bank.

Once appointed at the ripe old age of 32, Hamilton set about developing his organization. He appointed 39 people to help him run the Treasury Department more than any other Department in the newly formed government. The first thing Hamilton did was to focus on the issue of revenue for the Union. Hamilton started by creating a customs service that would operate at all American ports and collect the customs duties on goods coming from other countries. He called on his experience in St. Croix when he was in charge of the business for Cruger and Beekman and dealt with the ship captains who often were dishonest or tried to bypass paying any taxes on the goods they brought onto the island. In order to make sure that the laws were enforced and smuggling did not occur, Hamilton ordered that all lighthouses and beacons on the East Coast (there was no West Coast yet) be upgraded so that they could monitor incoming ship traffic. He also set up guard boats to patrol the ports. These guard boats were the foundation of the Coast Guard which now patrols the seas around the country. This was not one of Hamilton's top ten achievements but it was significant that he had the foresight to think about a service organization which would help keep America's shores safe.

The next thing Hamilton did was tackle the issue of debt. If you remember, the issue of debt had led to a rebellion of farmers and home owners who were losing their homes and properties. Shays' rebellion was still fresh in everyone's mind. In his characteristic way, Hamilton thought through what to do about this important issue and wrote an enormous report, *The Report on Public Credit*, in which he outlined what he proposed to do to deal with the debt that was plaguing the country. His solution was to get Congress to agree to assume all of the debt that had been accumulated during the Revolution (state and federal) and consolidate it into one entity, the public credit, which could issue bonds that could be bought and sold like any other commodity.

Of course, it was one thing to write a report; it was another to get everyone to agree to the concept and to pass a bill that would make the idea into a law. It was an entirely new idea. It also led to a lot of political wrangling between the Federalists and the anti-Federalists and highlighted the differences between the Northern states which were still mired in debt and the Southern States which had largely paid off their debts and weren't interested in buying into the idea of a national debt. Hamilton lobbied as best as he could but saw the chance for passage of his assumption bill (called the assumption bill because it dealt with the assumption of debt) dwindling by the day.

The impasse continued until there was finally a meeting of some of the great minds of the young country who worked out a deal. The deal was the brainchild of James Madison of Virginia, Thomas Jefferson of Virginia and Hamilton. We will look at how Jefferson played a role in Hamilton's life but for now, it is just important to know that Hamilton and Jefferson were on opposite sides of the political spectrum. Hamilton favored strong government while Jefferson, who like Washington was a wealthy landowner, favored a weak government and had a vision of the new Union remaining largely a nation of farmers. Jefferson and Madison were very powerful members of Congress and they were both from the South so they did not want their region assuming the debt that had been accumulated by the Northern States.

But Jefferson and Madison had an idea. They wanted to move the capital of the new country to their neck of the woods. Instead of being in New York, which Hamilton favored, the two wanted to move the capital to a spot along the Potomac River in Virginia which would in effect, move the power base into the South. The story goes that the three men met at Jefferson's house in New York City on a warm summer night in 1790 to discuss a possible deal. If Hamilton agreed to lobby for moving the capital, Jefferson and Madison would lobby for getting the assumption bill passed. Hamilton wanted New York to remain the capital but he was willing to sacrifice this if his bill could get passed. The deal was done. Hamilton got his bill passed; Madison and Jefferson got the capital to be in Virginia. But Jefferson later regretted doing the deal because he was a staunch believer in a decentralized model of government and Hamilton's assumption bill was another step toward a strong centralized government. Hamilton, Jefferson and Madison worked together to make this all happen. But it was the last time they would join forces to do anything.

After the assumption bill was passed, Hamilton continued to work on a central banking strategy for the country. Hamilton set up a system for collecting taxes and most importantly, a national bank. His bank bill was passed without much opposition and so the country had a central bank. Finally, Hamilton streamlined the currency system that was so disjointed. He wrote another report, *The Report on the Mint*, about establishing a standard currency for the United States. It was to be the dollar which replaced the widely circulating British pounds and coins. The dollar was to be either a gold or silver coin. Hamilton also devised a system for smaller coins based on the decimal system. Our coins, the quarter, dime, and penny, are all based on this system. Finally, there was some order in how Americans paid for goods.

In his time as Secretary of the Treasury, he had transformed the country in dramatic ways. There was a central bank, public credit, a currency system, a means for collecting taxes, and a customs service. These achievements would be part of Hamilton's lasting legacy. It is no wonder that the ten dollar bill has his face on it!

While Hamilton focused his efforts primarily on banking and setting up a strong central government, he also was involved in developing the manufacturing sector in the United States. Hamilton was way ahead of his time in beginning to dream about a new society in the United States which would be a robust economic engine powered by manufacturing. Up till now, Americans were overwhelmingly farmers who worked the land. Hamilton wanted the country to be able to compete on a world stage.

A good example was the textile industry in Britain which produced the bulk of the textile goods in the world. Also, British laws were

enacted which kept a tight rein on the exporting
of the machines used to manufacture textiles as
well as the trade secrets associated with the
industry. As a result, the colonists were forced to
buy most of their textile goods from Britain.
Hamilton decided to do something about this.
He started the New York Manufacturing Society.
This organization invested in a woolen factory in
Lower Manhattan. The facility was not successful
and closed after a few years because there was
not enough water power to run its machines. But
Hamilton was undaunted and saw the potential
of manufacturing. In May 1790, Hamilton and
his newly appointed assistant secretary of the
treasury, Tench Coxe, got together and decided
that the best way to get British knowhow on
textiles was to go after the managers of the

factories in Britain and entice them to come to the United States. Hamilton and Coxe succeeded in getting a man named Parkinson who was a British weaver, to come to America with his knowledge of how to set up a flax mill. This was illegal but the government looked the other way because they issued him patents for setting up the mill.

Hamilton then created the Society for Establishing Useful Manufactures (SEUM) in 1791 which was a private group dedicated to creating a pilot project in manufacturing. The society wanted to create not only a mill; it also wanted to create an entire factory town. The prospectus for the project listed a large number of goods which would be produced in this town including cottons, linens, thread, hats, ribbons, and blankets. Hamilton thought that if this business was successful, other businesses would follow its example and set up shop. The town was founded in New Jersey and called Paterson in honor of the Governor of New Jersey, William Paterson. Hamilton picked the particular spot because it had a natural waterfalls which would provide the power for the factory. Hamilton personally oversaw the recruitment of the first supervisors for the cotton mill. While this venture was not successful, it laid the foundation for other similar ventures.

Now that Hamilton had shown the American population that manufacturing was possible, he wrote a paper called *The Report on Manufactures* about how America could become a manufacturing giant. Not only did Hamilton want to encourage Americans to develop the industry, he also wanted to make sure that America would be self-sufficient if there was another war. Indeed, most of the goods used during the Revolutionary War including the soldier's uniforms, and other supplies, were imported. For *The Report*, Hamilton enlisted the help of Coxe and others to help him to develop ideas for the various aspects of the industry.

While this seemed to be a great idea, Hamilton knew that not everyone would get on board with him. There were many who wanted America to remain agrarian; it had lots of land and these people argued that a democracy could only thrive if it was based on farming. Thomas Jefferson was the chief advocate for this point of view as we noted earlier. We will return later to Jefferson and Hamilton and their relationship.

Hamilton also believed that there was nothing wrong in having a job in a factory. There would be more productivity, he claimed, because work could be divided into simple operations which could be later mechanized. One of the surprising ideas of Hamilton's was that child labor was okay. He thought that there was nothing wrong with having children and women participating in the workforce. He did not foresee the horrible working conditions that were forced on children and women in the factories in the industrial world later in the century; instead, he drew on his own experiences as young child working in the West Indies for Cruger and Beekman.

It is truly amazing that Hamilton laid the foundation for the industrial growth in the United States. He foresaw a rise in entrepreneurship which would in turn would lead to innovative ideas and better overall prosperity.  His ideas were the precursors of early factories in the United States and managerial models. While we may look upon these ideas as flawed, they were the impetus for a different kind of society that would be responsible for making the United States a world power.

Another incident happened while Hamilton was Secretary of the Treasury which showed that even though the country was on the right track with regard to finances, there was still a lot to do. The incident is called the Whiskey Rebellion. It all started when Hamilton decided to impose a tax on whiskey and other alcoholic beverages in order to raise revenues for the government. The farmers in Pennsylvania rebelled because they said that they used the wheat they grew to make whiskey and sell it. It was an old tradition in the hills of Pennsylvania to create what was called moonshine. Hamilton's tax created an uproar – now there were laws governing the sale of so-called moonshine. By 1792, the farmers had gotten more and more violent with regard to the tax. They were attacking the tax collectors and threatening them with bodily harm. Hamilton became alarmed and he told President Washington that he needed to use force to stop the farmers. Washington agreed and sent Hamilton with men from the militias of Virginia,

Maryland and New Jersey to stop the rebellion. Ultimately the rebellion was stopped but not before Hamilton tried to impose harsh penalties on the farmers. Hamilton was infuriated at the rebels and wanted them deported. Washington offered the farmers amnesty.

In December 1794, Hamilton told President Washington that he was going to resign as Secretary of the Treasury. He was tired, was needed at home and had been the subject of many attacks on his character. Soon after, in 1795, Hamilton resigned from his post as Secretary of the Treasury. But though he retired from his official capacity as a member of Washington's cabinet, he remained one of Washington's closest advisers. In fact, Washington called him back to help him out with a problem that had arisen between Britain and the United States. In 1794, John Jay had been sent to Britain to negotiate a treaty between the two countries regarding trade. The essence of the treaty was that Britain would stop seizing American ships that were sailing through the Caribbean. These ships were actually supplying France with arms and other supplies; France was at war with Britain and relied on the United States for help. The British would not yield on this point. However, they did agree to give America a most favored nation status which was a great boon to the economic prosperity of the country. This meant that there would be special status for goods that were exported from America to Britain and vice versa. Trade with Britain tripled during that time.

Though it had contributed to the development of the country's economy, the Jay Treaty was not well received by the majority of Americans. Hamilton, who endorsed the Treaty, tried to reason with people but was instead met with hatred. At a rally in New York City, he was pelted with rocks. The Jay Treaty was finally ratified by the Congress but it left its mark on the politics of the young country, not least of all a running battle between Washington's Federalists and Jefferson and his Anti-Federalists.

The next year, Washington decided not to run for a third term as President. Hamilton and Washington worked closely to draft Washington's farewell address to the country. It was their last collaborative effort and it reflected the philosophy that Americans should see themselves as part of one nation. Washington went back to Virginia in 1796 and Hamilton left government service at least for a while. John Adams was elected President in 1796.

The name Thomas Jefferson has been mentioned many times throughout this chapter and it is time to talk about him and who he was. There were many differences between Hamilton and Jefferson. They were both founders of the country and both contributed significantly. But they had different origins and they had differing views on some fundamental issues. It is impossible to provide a full blown portrait of Jefferson in this book. Instead, Jefferson's views and ideas will be used to provide a contrast with Hamilton's.

Some brief facts about Jefferson. He was appointed as Washington's Secretary of State at the same time that Hamilton became Secretary of the Treasury. Jefferson was a wealthy landowner from Virginia. He had received a first rate classical education and was considered to be a member of the Virginia aristocracy. He built a magnificent estate named Monticello and owned many slaves. He was a great advocate of the rural way of life as we have seen which was diametrically opposed to Hamilton's views.

Jefferson did play an important role in the Revolutionary War and is the author of the Declaration of Independence which was *the document* which officially proclaimed the colonies' independence from Britain on July 4, 1776. Like Hamilton, Jefferson had a gift for writing and his words were taken to heart by all of the patriots. Yet, there was a dark side to Jefferson's views on liberty. He owned slaves and his attitude toward slavery was so different than his attitude toward the lofty goals of liberty he wrote about in the Declaration of Independence.

In order to discuss this, it is important to review Hamilton's views on slavery. As we have seen, Hamilton was a lifelong opponent of slavery. These views continued to inform his actions throughout his career in the newly formed American government. The problem was that slavery was part of the American culture not only in the Southern States but also in the Northern States such as Vermont, New Hampshire, and Pennsylvania. In New York, slavery was also part of the picture. Slave auctions were held and many families in New York City kept slaves who served as cooks and servants. Owners of Hudson River estates had slaves who farmed the land. In early 1785, Hamilton and some other prominent people, established the New York Society for the Manumission of Slaves. The Society's goal was to show compassion toward the slaves but also help them to gain their freedom. Hamilton was at the forefront of these efforts and urged the members of Society and other people in New York to free their slaves.

On the other hand, Jefferson, who owned over 200 slaves, was less committed to their freedom. He was a great supporter of the Revolution and its stance on liberty for the colonists but when it came to slaves, he stopped short of endorsing their freedom. He thought that the problem would go away by itself over time and only freed a few of his slaves on his estate. James Madison also owned over 125 slaves and though he was very humane as a master, he was still a master and believed in the system that was supporting the economy of Virginia and the entire South.

After the War, as mentioned above, Jefferson was appointed Secretary of State by Washington. He did not like Hamilton and except for the deal which exchanged moving the capital for passing Hamilton's assumption bill, Jefferson never wanted to work with Hamilton. Increasingly, he and his Republican party went after Hamilton for a variety of things. Jefferson believed that Hamilton often manipulated Washington for his own ends. He also was very opposed to all of Hamilton's views on centralizing the government. When it came time to sign the Constitution, Jefferson sat on the fence for a while before he finally signed the document along with the other delegates at the Constitutional Convention.

Jefferson continued to be an important figure in the development of the new government. He became a leader of the Republican Party (the original Anti-Federalist party) which held very different views than the Federalists. During the battle in Congress about the Jay Treaty, Jefferson became increasingly angry and accused Washington of being a traitor. Washington, who had been warned about Jefferson's attitudes and ideas, refused to believe that Jefferson could turn against him. He had been such an important member of the government, had written the Declaration of Independence and had served as his Secretary of State. Finally, Washington severed his ties with Jefferson and would have nothing to do with him.

Meanwhile, President John Adams was dealing with a conflict with France. Jefferson and his party were very supportive of the French and the French Revolution. Hamilton while not involved in the day to day workings of the government, was concerned that the French were going to declare war on America. Adams disliked Hamilton and called him a 'bastard brat of a Scotch pedlar'. He also resented Hamilton's deep relationship with Washington.

In 1797, the French began to engage in open acts of war by seizing American ships and expelling America's ambassador to France. Adams sent a delegation to France which was ignored. When war seemed inevitable, Adams had no choice but to form an army. But who would lead it? Adams wanted Washington to lead the army but Washington would only agree if Hamilton was appointed as his second in command. Adams detested Hamilton; however, he had no choice but to agree to this. So Hamilton was appointed as Inspector General and Major General of the army. Adams and his Republican friends continued to accuse Hamilton of having too much influence on Washington and thought that the two men were conspiring to have Adams removed as President. While this was not true, it is clear that there were deep divisions among the founding fathers which often led to horrible arguments.

In any case, days after Hamilton was appointed, Adams decided to send another delegation to France. Adams was interested in making peace with France and this was accomplished. The French agreed to back down and war was averted. Hamilton put away his uniform but stayed involved in the political arena of the country.

The animosity between Adams and Hamilton continued and spilled into the election of 1800. Adams wanted to run for a second term and even though Adams was a Federalist, which was Hamilton's party, Hamilton did not want this to happen so Hamilton wrote a long paper condemning Adam's policies. He also supported a man named Thomas Pinckney. When Adams found out, he was outraged.

On the Republican side, two people were running for President – Thomas Jefferson and Aaron Burr. Hamilton did not want Jefferson to be President either so he wrote a series of essays in which he tried to discredit Jefferson. In any event, the election was held and Adams lost to Jefferson by eight electoral votes. But Jefferson did not automatically become the President of the United States. The Republicans thought that Burr would finish second and become the Vice President. Instead, Jefferson and Burr were tied in Electoral College votes. The only way to break the tie was to send it to the House of Representatives for a vote. Though Hamilton despised Jefferson, he decided to vote for him instead of Burr. He had already met with Burr several times and did not like him for a variety of reasons. After 26 ballots, Jefferson became the president and Burr, the vice president.

On becoming President, Jefferson was expected to get rid of most of Hamilton's infrastructure including the Bank which he had established. Instead, Jefferson did keep much of what Hamilton and the Federalists had created. He continued to despise Hamilton and had his Treasury Secretary, Albert Gallatin, go through Hamilton's files to see if he could find anything scandalous or imperfect about Hamilton's legacy.  But there was nothing wrong with what Hamilton had done much to Jefferson's disappointment.

There was one area of the government which Jefferson tried to destroy. That was the Judiciary system which had been created under Adams.

Under Adams, the Congress had enacted the Judiciary Act, which enabled the creation of the court system and twenty-three new federal judgeships. This was done so that the Supreme Court justices did not have to ride around to the different courts to decide cases. Remember that there were no paved roads and so the Justices would have had to ride around on dirt roads which were often muddy.

Adams appointed mostly judges who sided with the Federalists. The Republicans did not like this obviously. They especially did not like Adams' appointment of Chief Justice John Marshall who proved to be a great supporter of Hamilton's ideas. Jefferson hated Marshall and called him a snake! Jefferson tried to get Congress to repeal the Judiciary Act. Hamilton was appalled and wrote about the need to have a strong judiciary system. He saw Jefferson's efforts as the President's first efforts to destroy the Constitution. In the end, Jefferson was successful in getting the Act repealed.

Jefferson and Hamilton continued their feud with Hamilton accusing Jefferson of being a tyrant and pointed out that he had been reluctant to adopt the Constitution. He also wrote letters and other documents going after Jefferson's personal reputation. Jefferson for his part, stepped up his attacks on Hamilton. He tried to get Washington to side with him against Hamilton but Washington refused.

The dispute with Jefferson and Jefferson's views on many issues had a profound effect on Hamilton. The result was that he and some of his friends decided to establish a new Federalist newspaper called *The New York Evening Post* in 1801. Hamilton contributed some of his funds to help get the newspaper off the ground. Hamilton picked a man named William Coleman to the editor of *The Post* and set up shop on Pine Street in Lower Manhattan not far from Hamilton's home. Hamilton used the paper to expound on his views and published a series of essays called "The Examination". He felt that he had been put aside by Jefferson and his Republicans and this was a way to keep his so-called skin in the game.

In the next chapter, we will look at Hamilton's personal life. Along with being a family man, Hamilton did have an interesting and controversial love life.

## Chapter IV – Hamilton as Family Man and Lover

In earlier chapters, Hamilton was described as a man obsessed with the War and with making a name for himself as a statesman and leader. Indeed, these tasks did consume his time and often exhausted him. But there was another side to Hamilton that rounds out his personality and gives you a deeper understanding of how the man operated. Hamilton was a very good looking guy and throughout his career loved to have fun which in those years meant singing, dancing, and courting ladies. Above all, he was a family man with a large number of children. This chapter will look at his marriage to Eliza Schuyler as well as his affairs and relationships with various women.

First, we will look at his marriage to Eliza Schuyler. Our story begins in Morristown during the winter of 1780 where you will recall from Chapter II, Washington set up camp with his army. Hamilton was there too. It was a gloomy winter and Hamilton was looking for some distractions. He already had a reputation of being a flirt. In fact, Martha Washington, the General's wife, nicknamed her amorous tomcat "Hamilton". In between fighting battles, Hamilton flirted with the ladies who would stop by the army's headquarters. He enjoyed dancing and having a good time with the "camp ladies" as they were called.

Throughout the winter of 1780, which was one of the most frigid in memory, Hamilton was able to pursue his passion for entertainment. There were sleighing parties and fancy dress balls attended by the army officers. Hamilton enjoyed himself immensely at these events and courted a few ladies. One of them was a woman named Cornelia Lott. Washington and his friends were amused by Hamilton's advances toward Ms. Lott. Later in the winter, he went after a woman named Polly. Yes, he was a fickle man and showed no signs of settling down.

Hamilton told a friend that he was wedded to the army; nevertheless, he began to think of marriage in 1779, and wrote to his friend John Laurens about his thinking. Of course Hamilton had been the product of an extremely unhappy marriage so he was very uneasy about picking a wife and being in a lifelong relationship. He also had very high standards for what he was looking for in a wife. She had to be beautiful, intelligent, and of good character. He also recognized that he needed someone who had money. Though he was not greedy, he felt that it was important for his future wife to have money so she could indulge in whatever things she wanted to acquire or do. So Hamilton had his criteria for what constituted his mate for life.

Into the picture came Eliza Schuyler, the daughter of Phillip Schuyler, one of the wealthiest men in the Hudson Valley. She came to Morristown in February to stay with relatives. Her aunt Gertrude had married Dr. John Cochran who had moved to New Jersey. Cochran was Washington's personal physician and later became the director of the Continental Army's medical department.  Eliza was going to stay with the Cochrans. As it happens, Hamilton had already met Eliza in Albany in 1777 when he was engaged in persuading General Gates to surrender some of his troops.  He had not been all that impressed with her at the time. But this was about to change.

Eliza was accompanied not only by a military escort but also by a woman named Kitty Livingston who Hamilton had already flirted with. Hamilton was 25 and fell in love with Eliza. He became a frequent visitor at the Cochran residence throughout the winter.  People began to notice that the normally "together" Hamilton was becoming absent-minded and often was seen lost in thought as he wandered around Morristown. He had found the woman of his dreams.

By the time he left Morristown in March, he and Eliza had decided to get married. Eliza was not only beautiful; she fulfilled all of Hamilton's criteria for a wife including being a member of a wealthy family. Eliza became an important influence on Hamilton's life as we shall see. She was known as someone who was good natured, kind, and charming. She was also athletic and was an avid walker. Eliza had gotten little formal education but she had accompanied her father Phillip on some of his diplomatic missions so she had been exposed to politics and public affairs. She was very interested in exploring her surroundings and was by no means just a pretty face.

Hamilton lost no time getting to know the Schuylers who lived in Albany. It was a large family with three sons and five daughters. He even wrote to Eliza's sibling Peggy about his love for her sister, who he called Eliza or Betsey. He also was very attracted to Angelica, Eliza's older married sister and spent the rest of his life in a kind of Platonic relationship with her. Angelica was a different kind of person than Eliza. She was more playful, more fun to be with than Eliza. She played the guitar and loved to discuss books and current affairs.

He spent all of 1780 courting Eliza with endless letters and poems. Eliza was very taken by his great mind, his wit, and his good heart. She too was in love. But there was the issue of her father. General Phillip Schuyler was well aware that Hamilton was not 'one of them'. He was outside of their social circle and Schuyler would be taking a great risk if the two got married. Schuyler was a member of a family which had mingled with the other aristocrats of the Hudson Valley and he himself had married Catherine van Rensselaer, the heiress to the Claverack estate in Columbia County. But some of his other daughters had also married outside the clan so to speak. Angelica had married a gentleman named John Barker Church who was from England and who had a questionable history. Some said he had fled to America to escape from a duel in which he had killed someone. The couple eloped and Schuyler took a long time to accept his new son-in-law. Schuyler sized up Hamilton and decided that he could do worse for his daughter. Hamilton was not an aristocrat but he was clearly a brilliant man and would be a good husband. Hamilton was also a distinguished soldier and well connected to Washington. Schuyler and his wife moved down to Morristown to oversee the relationship between Eliza and Hamilton. Every evening, Hamilton would go over to their house and spend time with them.

In February, Hamilton asked for Eliza's hand in marriage. In those years, it was customary to ask for a woman's hand in marriage from her father. General Schuyler gave his consent to the marriage. On December 14, 1780, Alexander Hamilton and Eliza Schuyler were married at the

Schuyler mansion in Albany. It was a small wedding. Hamilton contacted his father who was still in the West Indies but he did not come. Nor did his brother James.

Many people viewed this improbable marriage of Alexander Hamilton, an immigrant from the West Indies, as an opportunity for Hamilton to marry into money and become a member of the aristocracy instantaneously. However, Hamilton did not think like that and surprisingly asked Eliza in one of his letters whether she would be willing to give up her rich life for one that was much more restrained with fewer luxuries. Clearly, Hamilton was ecstatic that he had met someone as wonderful as Eliza. Having been deprived of a family in his youth, he had now married into one and he loved that idea.

Schuyler ended up having a wonderful relationship with his new son-in-law. Hamilton was welcomed into the household. Hamilton and Schuyler shared many views on the War and how the country should be set up after the War. Like Hamilton, Schuyler was less than fond of the Articles of Confederation and wanted them to be stronger.  He also told Hamilton that he should respond to any personal attacks and believed in a kind of code of honor like his son-in-law.  After the wedding, in January 1781, Hamilton went back to his military duties and Betsey stayed in Albany. She was pregnant with their first child, Phillip.

After the battle of Yorktown, Hamilton went to Albany to be at the birth of his son, Phillip was born on January 22, 1782. He was the first of eight children that Eliza and Alexander were to have. The Hamiltons also adopted a child named Fanny who was the daughter of a Revolutionary War veteran who had suffered a nervous breakdown following the death of his wife. While he remained deeply involved in the War effort, Hamilton loved being a father. He doted on his children and was very concerned with them. He especially cared about their manners. He made sure they were educated but was apparently more concerned with their grades than with what they actually learned. He had high hopes for his firstborn son Phillip who continued to delight him. Hamilton hoped that Phillip would follow in his father's footsteps.

Eliza was in charge of the children's education and she also believed in providing religious instruction to the children. Hamilton hired tutors to teach his children French and all of them were fluent in the language.

Toward Eliza, he was very affectionate but he was also torn between his love for her and his affection for her sister Angelica. As noted earlier, Hamilton had a very special relationship with Angelica and some people have speculated that had she been available, he would have proposed to her and married her instead of Eliza. Angelica had married John Barker Church who was not the most handsome man in the world. However, he was a great businessman and became very wealthy. His business included contracts to sell supplies to the American and French forces. Yet Church was apparently a very cold person and did not have the intellectual capabilities that Hamilton had.

No one really knows how far the relationship between Hamilton and his sister-in-law really went. Angelica returned the affection to Hamilton but curiously, Eliza did not seem to mind this relationship. Hamilton was clearly infatuated with Angelica but tried to keep from going over the edge regarding her. When she left with her husband to go to London in 1785, he was very despondent about this. Nevertheless, he made sure that Eliza knew how much he loved her. Was Hamilton a two timer in his own adopted family? Did he have a so-called menage a trois with the two sisters? It is hard to say. Angelica Church stayed in London with her husband and her four children for many years.

The Churches finally returned to New York in 1797. Angelica and her husband were very active in the New York social scene and gossip certainly surfaced about Hamilton's continual adoration of his sister-in-law.

If you remember, Hamilton got his assumption bill passed because he made a deal with Jefferson and Madison to move the capital permanently to Virginia at a site near the Potomac River.  Hamilton hoped that New York would be the temporary capital while the new one was being built. Instead, the Pennsylvania and Virginia delegates decided that Philadelphia would be the temporary capital. So in 1791, with the capital of the country moving to Philadelphia, Hamilton had no choice but to move his family to Philadelphia. It was here that he had an affair that was probably the first sex scandal in American history.

Before getting to the scandal, it's a good idea to understand what was going on in Philadelphia. Most people today do not think of Philadelphia as a hip, exciting city. Yet in 1791, Philadelphia was believe it or not, a faster and more hip city than New York. There were constant parties and balls. Abigail Adams, John Adams' wife, was appalled at the way women dressed in Philadelphia. Women walked around with exposed arms and legs and often wore dresses showing off their bosoms. While today we accept this kind of display as normal, in those times it was considered pretty risqué. Eliza attended the parties with her husband but in May 1791, she decided to leave the city with her children and go back to Albany for the summer to stay with her father. There were horrible epidemics raging in Philadelphia and Phillip Schuyler wanted his daughter and her children to be safe.

Hamilton was now left to his own devices in Philadelphia. Hamilton, as we saw earlier in the chapter, always loved the company of women and now he was in Philly without his wife for a whole summer! Hamilton had already gotten a reputation for being a womanizer. To be fair to him, he never had time to relax and was always working. So maybe he saw his relationships with women as a diversion. He also was the son of a woman who had become an outcast in society and so in response, treated women with great respect. In fact, Hamilton used his office to help women who were in trouble. In one case, he helped a woman named Martha Walker who had petitioned the Congress because she claimed that her husband had enlisted in the Revolution and neglected valuable property that he owned before he enlisted. Hamilton wrote to Walker that he would help her in any way possible. He was always ready to help a woman in distress and this was to be his undoing.

Okay. Back to the scandal. While Hamilton in Philadelphia, a woman named Maria Reynolds appeared on the scene. She was 23 and was married to a guy named James Reynolds. Reynolds was a riverboat captain during the War. After the War, he became a speculator and lost a lot of money. Since he had lost so much money, he pushed Maria into becoming a prostitute. She conducted her business in their bedroom.

By many accounts, Reynolds was quite beautiful. She was poor, uneducated, and in a bad marriage so her gentlemen clients offered her a way out of a bad situation. She might not have been gorgeous but she was evidently more enticing than Hamilton's wife Eliza. She apparently had a way about her which Hamilton could not resist.

The story which Hamilton eventually told everyone was that Mrs. Reynolds, who probably had heard about Hamilton's womanizing tendencies, knocked on his door one evening. This was before Eliza and her family went to Albany for the summer. Hamilton let her into his home and took her to a part of the house where his family could not see her. Reynolds then began to tell him a horrible story about how she had been mistreated by her husband and how he had left her for another woman. She complained that she was penniless and appealed to Hamilton to help her. She was so persuasive that Hamilton fell for it, hook, line and sinker. He listened to her story and told her that he could not help her at the moment but that he would come to her house later that evening and bring her a small sum of money.

Unbeknownst to Eliza and the rest of his family, Hamilton went to Mrs. Reynolds' home that evening with some money. Of course, Mrs. Reynolds wanted more than just money and Hamilton obliged. These sexual encounters between Hamilton and Reynolds continued. Over and over again, Hamilton left his home during the late evening hours and spent time with Maria Reynolds. Once Eliza and the children went to Albany, he and Maria met and conducted this torrid affair in Hamilton's bedroom.

It is hard to understand what possessed Hamilton to engage in such a sordid affair. Perhaps he could not help himself. Perhaps he was not satisfied with Eliza and saw her only as mother of his children and did not find her sexually attractive. In any case, Hamilton continued the affair until one day, Reynolds announced to him that she and her husband James had reconciled. Hamilton later claimed that he had encouraged Maria to go back to her husband. In any case, Maria also told him that her husband was getting tips from the Treasury

Department and those tips had been profitable for him. Soon after Maria told him about her husband, he appeared at Hamilton's door and asked for a job at the Treasury Department. Hamilton refused to give him one.

For such an intelligent man, it is amazing that Hamilton did not see the writing on the wall about this whole affair. He was clearly going to be used by this couple and blackmailed. The problem was that Hamilton believed that Mrs. Reynolds loved him. He himself was most likely gripped by some dark sexual compulsion and could not stop himself though he admitted later that he tried to stop.

Maria played on Hamilton's feelings and continued to send letters about being desperate and needing money. Hamilton was a sucker for responding to women in need and he continued to give her money. He was never sure if she and her husband had conspired against him or whether she had acted alone. Hamilton vowed to get out of this horrible relationship but every time he tried to, Maria would play up her desperate situation and tell him that her husband was abusing her or that she would tell Eliza of the affair. Of course, Hamilton kept digging himself deeper into a hole from which he could not extract himself. While all of this was going on, Hamilton was sending love letters to Eliza. Eliza believed him and continued to worship him. She never suspected that he was engaged in such a disastrous affair.

Late in December 1791, Maria Reynolds turned up the heat. She wrote to Hamilton that her husband was threatening to reveal everything to Eliza. If this wasn't bad enough, James wrote another note in which he told Hamilton that he had known from the beginning that his wife was involved with Hamilton and that he Hamilton had taken advantage of his wife. He wrote angrily that Hamilton had made his life miserable and that he was now forced to take his daughter with him and leave Maria. Hamilton had no choice but to confront James.

When Hamilton did confront James, Hamilton asked him what evidence he had about the affair and Reynolds could not produce anything concrete. However, it was clear that Hamilton would have to pay this man something to keep the whole thing quiet. Hamilton agreed to pay Reynolds 1000 dollars which does not seem like a lot of money. However, for Hamilton who was making around 3500 dollars a year, it was an enormous sum. Still, he did not want anyone to find out about what had happened.

After Reynolds was paid and left, Hamilton decided that he had to stay away from Maria. James realized that his 'gravy train' might be at an end and wrote a letter to Hamilton telling him that he should come to the house and consider Maria his 'friend'. Instead of ending the affair, Hamilton succumbed to his basest instincts and went to see Maria again. The next day, James sent a note to Hamilton in which he demanded money to keep quiet about what the two 'lovers' were doing. This cycle continued with Maria writing letters pleading with Hamilton to come and Hamilton agreeing. The husband would then demand payment to keep the affair quiet. What a mess!

Things got even worse for Hamilton when Mr. Reynolds teamed up with a man named Jacob Clingman. Clingman had been a clerk for Frederick Muhlenberg, a congressman from Pennsylvania. Clingman had no scruples at all. He persuaded Reynolds to collaborate with him on a scheme to defraud the estate of a Revolutionary War veteran. The scheme was discovered and though Clingman went free on bail, Reynolds was put in jail for the crime.

Clingman needed to get the charges about this whole affair dropped so he went to Muhlenberg and told him about Hamilton's affair. Muhlenberg, who was a Republican, could not resist taking down Hamilton so he went to James

Monroe and Abraham Venable, two powerful Virginians who were well connected in the Republican Party. The three men went to see Maria Reynolds and assured her that Hamilton would never engage in such an affair. Maria told them that she doubted Hamilton was above participating in such an affair. The three men – Muhlenberg, Venable, and Monroe - then went to Hamilton to discuss the affair. Hamilton confessed to the men and thought that the entire affair would go away. However, these three men were certainly not Hamilton's friends. Monroe was especially out to get him. Monroe was a close friend of Jefferson, who we have already seen, despised Hamilton. This was not the end of Hamilton's troubles concerning his disastrous affair with Maria Reynolds.

If you remember, after Washington retired, there was a general election for President in 1796. Hamilton tried everything he knew to discredit Adams and Jefferson. After the election, in which Adams became President and Jefferson became Vice President, the two men did not forget what Hamilton had done. They vowed to get back at Hamilton and they did. Jefferson turned to one of his unsavory acquaintances to do the dirty work. His name was James Callender. Callender published a notice about a pamphlet in which he claimed that the letters from Reynolds proved that Hamilton had embezzled money from the Treasury. Of course, he had made up these charges but Callender did not care. Hamilton was infuriated and responded with a series of letters in which he denied the charges. He also insisted that Reynolds had thought up the whole scheme in order to get himself out of jail.

Hamilton was faced with the demise of his career and his reputation so he confessed the whole sordid thing. He wrote a pamphlet in which he described the affair in great detail and published all the letters he received from Maria and her husband. It was astonishing that he would do something like this. When the pamphlet came out, everyone was appalled. People who liked him did not know what to think. Hamilton had not only confessed to adultery. He had made it clear that the money he paid to Reynolds was for sex with his wife. Hamilton thought that by writing the pamphlet, he would be able to preserve his reputation. But that was not the case. The Federalists were shocked and the

Republicans rejoiced because finally they had brought down their greatest enemy. Thomas Jefferson wrote that the fact that Hamilton had chosen to admit his adultery strengthened the case that he was in fact guilty. John Adams and his wife both had suspected that Hamilton was a womanizer and this pamphlet confirmed their suspicions.

Hamilton was outraged and wrote to the three men to repudiate whatever Callender had written. Muhlenberg and Venable obliged but Monroe stalled. Monroe was staying in New York down the street from Hamilton and Hamilton requested an interview with Monroe to settle the issue. Monroe agreed and Hamilton went to Monroe's house with John Church, his sister-in-law's husband. Monroe invited a man named

David Gelston, a Republican bigwig. Gelston wrote about the encounter. He described how Hamilton was enraged and how he asked Monroe if he had leaked the Reynolds papers to Callender. Monroe countered that he knew nothing about the publication of the papers; he had been in Europe and did not know about what Callender had done until he returned. Hamilton accused Monroe of being a liar and Monroe reacted by calling Hamilton a scoundrel. The result of this confrontation was that Hamilton felt that his honor was at stake and he challenged Monroe to a duel. Monroe accepted. According to Gelston, the two men starting fighting with one another and had to be separated.  Gelston suggested that Monroe should meet with Venable and Muhlenberg and then get back to Hamilton about the whole business. Though he was still agitated, Hamilton agreed.

Lots of letters went back and forth between the two men. Hamilton was never satisfied. Though Venable and Muhlenberg agreed that they had accepted the story about Reynolds and were no longer pursuing the issue of Hamilton's wrongdoings at the Treasury, Hamilton wanted Monroe to denounce whatever Callender had said and admit that he was the one who had originally given the Reynolds paper and story to Callender. Monroe refused but did not want the dispute with Hamilton to escalate any further. Indeed, Hamilton and Monroe were ready to duel if necessary. Something had to be done and Monroe turned to his friend Aaron Burr to be the mediator between the two men. Monroe gave Burr Hamilton's letters on the issue. Monroe wrote a letter to Hamilton in which he wrote that he had no intentions of having a duel with him. The letter was delivered by Burr and Hamilton backed down at least for the moment. It is interesting that Burr did not egg on Monroe to fight with Hamilton. He could have set up a duel between the two men; but he decided against it.

Hamilton was not through with the issue and in August, he published another pamphlet about the issue. Instead of ignoring this, Monroe thought his honor was at stake and sent an angry letter to Hamilton in which he stated that Hamilton should have been satisfied with the previous discussions on the matter or invited him (Monroe) to a duel. Hamilton accepted the challenge and wrote a note to Monroe but never sent it. So the duel never happened and the matter was dropped.

As to his own party, the Federalists, the scandal might have tarnished his reputation a bit but for the most part, they still supported him. Washington sent a note and the gift of a wine cooler. The note seemed to indicate his solidarity with Hamilton and showed how he still had great respect for his right hand man.

The question remains as to how Eliza and his family figured into the Reynolds affair. Eliza was pregnant with the couple's sixth child. She had suffered an earlier miscarriage and this child was her first in five years. Apparently, Hamilton delayed the publication of his tell-all pamphlet about the Reynolds affair until after the child was born.

When the pamphlet was published, the Republican press attacked Eliza and wrote that Hamilton had violated the trust of his wife by engaging in this affair. If she had any thoughts about the affair, she never made them public. Despite Hamilton's horrible actions, Eliza remained loyal to her husband. Perhaps, she had concluded that it was worth suffering through these scandals because her marriage to Hamilton was so important and that Hamilton had compensated for his horrendous behavior by being a great husband in other ways. In fact, throughout her life and after Hamilton's death, Eliza never betrayed her love for her husband and always believed that he was a great patriot and that he had been slandered by his enemies. Hamilton in turn, wrote a series of letters to Eliza in which he professed his love for her. The love between these two people is one of the great early American love stories. That Eliza stood by her man is incredible to some of us. But it also shows that she truly loved him and was willing to forgive him despite his transgressions.

There was another incident in which it was clear that despite his affair with Maria Reynolds, he was still a family man. A couple of weeks after the infamous pamphlet was published, Hamilton's eldest son, Phillip became very ill. Hamilton was busy with court cases but rushed to be with Phillip and nursed him around the clock. Phillip did survive and Hamilton and Eliza breathed a sigh of relief. Clearly, Hamilton did not want to abandon his family and still remained devoted to them.

This man was a bundle of contradictions. On the one hand, he was so self-involved that he was ready to die for a slight to his honor. The Reynolds affair showed that he had a fiery temper and that he had considerable character weaknesses especially when it came to women. On the other hand, Hamilton truly loved his wife and his family and was willing to go to any lengths to make sure that his family stayed together and was well.

If you remember, Hamilton and his friends established a new Federalist paper in 1801 called *The New York Evening Post*. Just a week after the first issue of *The Post* was published, an event occurred which changed Hamilton's life and his family's life forever. His eldest son Phillip who was Hamilton's protégé and the son whom he hoped would follow in his footsteps, got into trouble. Phillip did follow his father in his career trajectory. He was a smart young man who went to Columbia College, the new name of King's College, and was studying to become a lawyer like his father. Also like his father, Phillip liked to have a good time and sometimes got into scrapes which necessitated his father's intervention. Hamilton tried to curb Phillip's tendencies by setting up a strict schedule for him which included writing, reading, and attending church. Hamilton loved his son but thought he was naughty.

As in other years, the Fourth of July celebration in 1801 was exciting in New York. There were lots of people having a good time at the celebration. One of them, a young lawyer named George Eaker, who sided with the Republicans, gave a speech to the assembled crowd. He talked about the war that had never happened – the Quasi-War it was called – with the French in 1798 and instead of blaming the French who had in fact, provoked the Americans by seizing ships, he blamed Hamilton and said that Hamilton had formed an army to frighten Republicans about a possible invasion by the French. He also said that it was Jefferson who had saved the Constitution and the government by chasing out the Federalists.

Phillip read the speech after it was published and took offense to what Eaker had said about his father. Phillip could not contain his anger and decided to do something about it. He and a friend named Price confronted Eaker while he was attending the theater. They started to taunt him about what he had spoken about on the Fourth. Eaker was very insulted and called the two men rascals which was a word that was used for provoking the other side into a duel. Phillip and Eaker started to fight and after they were separated by friends, Eaker told Phillip that he expected to hear from him. Phillip did not hesitate and soon after sent a letter to Eaker challenging him to a duel.

Phillip then consulted with John Church, Angelica's husband. Church told Phillip that he should respond to the insulting behavior of Eaker but that he should try to settle it without a duel. Phillip, who probably shared his father's code of honor, decided to go through with the duel.

Hamilton apparently knew about the duel but did not know what to do to prevent it. As we have seen, Hamilton was bound by a code of honor. He had almost dueled with Monroe over his honor. On the other hand, he was beginning to believe that dueling might not be the answer to resolving a conflict. And it was his own son who was defending his father's reputation. He counseled his son to refuse to fire first or waste his shot by firing into the air.  There was no guarantee that Eaker would not shoot him before Phillip could in effect miss.

Phillip borrowed pistols from Church, and the two duelists with their assistants, known as seconds, met on a sandbar near what is now

Jersey City. Phillip followed his father's advice and did not shoot. At first, Eaker did not shoot either. But then, he raised his pistol, Phillip raised his pistol and Eaker shot Phillip above his right hip. The bullet went through Phillip's body. Phillip was rushed across the river to Manhattan where doctors came immediately. But they could not save Phillip and he died the next morning. Eliza, who was pregnant with their eighth child, was devastated as was Alexander. They named the newly born son Phillip after their firstborn.

After the death of his son, Hamilton wrote a series of articles for *The Post* about the duel in which he told the readers that Eaker had been the villain in the affair. It was Eaker, Hamilton claimed, who had murdered his son because he had fired at him when Phillip had no intentions of firing back. Eaker pointed out that Phillip had provoked him at the theater and that he had agreed to the duel. Phillip had brought a pistol to the duel and had raised his pistol when Eaker did. Eaker was never tried for Phillip Hamilton's death and died two years later.

The family was shattered by Phillip's death. One of Hamilton's daughters, Angelica, who was 17 at the time, had a mental breakdown as a result of the death of her brother. Hamilton did not retreat from public life and continued to write and to take cases. He also decided to spend more time with his family and bought some property in upper Manhattan where he built a home for his family. He called the place The Grange in honor of his grandparents' home in Scotland as well as that of his Uncle James' place in St. Croix.

Hamilton became more involved with his family and spent part of his time learning how to garden. He also spent a lot of money on the house and on landscaping the property. Onto the next chapter, where Hamilton fights with Burr and loses his life.

# Chapter V – Hamilton vs. Burr

When we last left Alexander Hamilton, he was a shattered man. Though he still participated in politics, the death of Hamilton's son had a lasting effect on him. He decided to devote more time to his family and set up a family homestead in upper Manhattan. It sounds like he had finally settled down. But, if you think about how driven Hamilton was by his career goals and his character, then you will understand the final chapter of his life. Everyone has an opinion about why Hamilton risked everything and ended up dying from wounds he suffered in a duel that he fought with Aaron Burr.

To give you a better understanding of what led up to the famous duel in New Jersey on July 12, 1804, between Alexander Hamilton and Aaron

Burr, it is worthwhile going back to some of the history of the relationship between these two men, a history which led up to the fateful day in 1804. In many ways, they led parallel lives which periodically intersected in good and bad ways.

Aaron Burr was born in 1754. He was the son of Reverend Aaron Burr Senior, who was the President of the College of New Jersey, later Princeton University. Burr Senior met his wife, Esther, in Northampton, Massachusetts. She was the daughter of Jonathan Edwards, a hellfire and damnation preacher. The two fell in love and married. Esther had two children with Burr Senior – Sarah and Aaron. Aaron was a sickly child; however, his parents thought that he was clever and mischievous.

Aaron Burr grew up during the French and Indian War. His father died at the age of 42 and his mother later died of small pox. So much like Alexander Hamilton, Aaron Burr was orphaned at a young age. He and his sister, nicknamed Sally, went to live with a Dr. Shippen, who made sure they had a tutor. Aaron eventually was shipped off to Elizabethtown Academy in New Jersey where he flourished. You might remember that this was the same place that Hamilton attended for his early education after leaving the West Indies. After only two years at the Academy, Aaron Burr decided that he was ready to apply to Princeton where his father had been President. He applied at the age of eleven and was immediately rejected. Burr was undaunted and on his own, studied the first two years of the Princeton College curriculum. He then reapplied and even though he should have been admitted as a junior, he was admitted as a sophomore. He still graduated at the age of 15, which is truly astonishing.

During his time at Princeton, Burr distinguished himself in his studies but like his future adversary, he was a ladies man and was often seen amusing himself by chasing after one woman or another. He apparently had many sexual conquests and affairs. After graduating from Princeton, Burr spent the next year "goofing off". He was not sure what career to follow so he spent his time hanging out and having some notorious affairs. Finally, he decided to go for the Ministry but after a few months of studying for this career, Burr got bored and decided to become a lawyer. This was the beginning of Burr's long and distinguished career first as a lawyer and then as a legislator and member of the inner circle of founding fathers.

Here's the first intersection of Hamilton and Burr's lives. If you recall, in Chapter I, there was a man named Hugh Knox, who played an enormous role in Hamilton's life. For it was Knox who read Hamilton's essay on the hurricane in St. Croix and raised money for him to go to New York. Also, if you remember, Knox had come to the West Indies because Aaron Burr's father had sent him there. Knox certainly must have mentioned the name Aaron Burr to Hamilton.

Like Hamilton, Burr hesitated about getting into the Revolutionary War effort but finally joined the fight after the battle of Lexington and Concord. Burr was a fearless soldier and was assigned to go on a mission with Benedict Arnold and other men to take Quebec from the British. It was a disastrous affair and ended with the deaths of many of the men. Burr survived and distinguished himself there as a soldier and leader. Burr thought that Washington would now recognize him and give him a promotion and a great command.

But he was wrong. Instead of rewarding him for his valor, Washington promoted him and sent him to a regiment that had been privately funded by a man named William Malcolm. Malcolm assigned Burr to train the recruits. Burr was bored and angry with this assignment and maybe this was the seed of his resentment toward Washington and his able assistant Hamilton. Burr did train the recruits and eventually commanded them as they fought the British in a small skirmish in what is now Bergen County. Again Burr distinguished himself and again Washington ignored him. Burr's next assignment in 1778, was to preside over the Neutral territory in Westchester County. No glory for him! Burr, who had various illnesses, spent much of his time in Westchester in bed. Finally, in 1779, after a less than distinguished career, Burr resigned from the army.

From Burr's point of view, the only positive thing that happened while he was in Westchester was that he met a beautiful woman named Theodosia

Prevost. Theodosia was a very educated woman but she also suffered from various ailments. Theodosia was married and to an Englishman no less. He was a Captain when Theodosia married him and after a stint in New Jersey and Georgia, Captain Prevost was sent to the British West Indies to be a lieutenant governor of one of the islands there. Theodosia refused to go with her husband and remained in New Jersey where she met Burr. To complicate matters, the Prevosts had five children as well. The island Prevost was sent to was not Nevis or St. Croix but it is a bit uncanny that Burr's life was changed by the islands where Hamilton grew up. Because her husband was stationed in that god-forsaken part of the world, Burr was free to pursue his lover and have a torrid affair with her much of it secretly. Eventually, the lieutenant governor died of yellow fever while in the Islands and Theodosia and Burr were married.

It was after the War that Hamilton and Burr came into real contact with one another. They both moved with their families to New York City. Burr brought his wife and her five children and also had another child with Theodosia was born in 1784 and was named Theodosia in honor of her mother. Burr lived lavishly and dreamed of having a country estate. His dreams were held in check by his wife but he always seemed to be in debt because he was a big spender. Hamilton on the other hand lived more modestly with his family.

Both men were lawyers in New York City which was emerging as a center of commerce and wealth. There were plenty of cases to go around since most of the British lawyers had all left the city. Hamilton and Burr became the two most prominent lawyers in the city. They had different styles. Hamilton was flamboyant and quite an orator who would go on and on about an issue. Burr was not as flamboyant and was quite terse in the way he talked during court appearances. He was very dispassionate compared to what we have seen of Hamilton who was a fiery man who could command an audience whether as a writer or as a speaker. Hamilton was also very good looking while Burr was not the most handsome man and not nearly as dashing as Hamilton. Burr needed money and took any case that came his way. He charged more money for a case than any other lawyer in the city and many of his clients were from New York's aristocracy.

Hamilton on the other hand, was less interested in money and took cases that interested him and that were significant because of the kinds of subjects they addressed. If you recall, Hamilton was widely criticized because he took on cases that involved the return of property to the Tories who had fled to England.

The next point where Burr and Hamilton interacted was in the New York Assembly. Burr had never been interested in politics but in 1784, a man named Alexander McDougall named him to a slate of candidates who would represent New York in the Assembly. Burr was not very excited about this opportunity but he did serve in the Assembly and was re-elected for a second term. Hamilton, who also was not actively seeking office, was drafted to the Assembly and so the two men met in Albany.

However, like Burr, Hamilton was not really interested in New York's issues. As we have seen, he was more interested in what was happening on a national level. He was involved in arguing about and writing the Constitution of the United States. At that point, Burr was apparently on the sidelines regarding the Constitution. However, he did side with the Anti-Federalists, which put him on a collision course with Hamilton.

After the Constitution was ratified, Hamilton worked for Washington who was elected President. Meanwhile, Burr was appointed to be New York Governor George Clinton's Attorney General. Though the position of Attorney General for the State of New York was relatively obscure, Burr still was able to keep his hand in politics. His chance came when the New York Assembly had to decide who would occupy the State's Senate seat. Hamilton had maneuvered through the political minefield that characterized New York politics and made some mistakes. But he expected his father-in-law, Phillip Schuyler, who had held one of the seats for two years, to be chosen by the Assembly. Instead, when the vote came up, Aaron Burr was elected over Schuyler. Hamilton was furious and held a grudge against Burr for outsmarting him. From Hamilton's point of view, Burr was not a principled man and he rarely took positions on important issues of the day.

Despite the fact that Hamilton became Secretary of the Treasury, and therefore had enormous power, he was haunted by other men in power such as Thomas Jefferson and James Madison who he believed were trying to discredit him every time he made a proposal. Moreover, Jefferson and Madison had aligned themselves with Burr and wanted Burr to help them with their campaign against Hamilton. Hamilton feared Burr and resented him not just because he had won the Senate seat from his father-in-law but also because he thought that this very smug person could one day rise in power above him. Already, some people were talking about Burr becoming a Vice President. Though it was presumed that Washington would hold office as long as he wanted to, his Vice President, John Adams, was not so secure. Burr's name kept coming up in the discussions about who would succeed Adams. Ultimately, Burr was not the nominee from the Republican Party; it was George Clinton, the Governor of New York. When the election was held in 1792, Washington was easily re-elected and Adams remained as his Vice President.

It was during the election of 1796 that Hamilton and Burr again clashed.  On the Federalist side, most people believed that Adams would succeed Washington. However, Hamilton supported someone else, a man named Thomas Pinckney, who was the Governor of South Carolina. Though he tried to keep everyone from knowing who he was backing, Burr, who was also maneuvering for at least a Vice Presidential spot, found out about Hamilton's choice and told Adams about it. Adams was furious and when he was elected, he retained all of Washington's cabinet except for Hamilton, who he felt had betrayed him. Burr, by the way, did not get to be the Vice President. He ran against Jefferson for the office and lost.

As the story of Hamilton and his relationship continued to unfold, it became increasingly clear that these two men would never see eye to eye on anything. They were so different in their politics and the way they conducted their personal lives. After Burr lost his bid for Vice President, he retreated back to New York and began to speculate on real estate. Burr was not a good investor and he got into big financial trouble. He partnered with a guy named James Greenleaf and the two bought a tract of land in upstate New York. Greenleaf was supposed to pay half of the amount for the land which was about 24,000 pounds (People were still using pounds to do transactions). However, Greenleaf reneged on the deal and the result was that Burr had to cough up his share of the money as well as Greenleaf's. Of course, he did not have the money and the owner of the property, one John Angerstein, sued him and hired none other than Alexander Hamilton to represent him. He did take Angerstein as his client and prosecuted Burr. Hamilton was amazed at how much Burr owed. Finally, unable to pay off his debts, Burr sold everything he owned and took a mortgage against his house. The once mighty Burr was now impoverished.

Burr left the Senate when his term ended, took a seat in the New York Assembly and went to live in upstate New York. He was down and out but not finished with being a schemer and a player in New York politics. One of his schemes was the creation of what was called the Manhattan Water Company. The company was created to provide water for the citizens of New York. Burr wanted the company to be a neutral entity and above the partisan politics of the Federalists and the Republicans. To do this, he enlisted the help of people from both parties to become members of a committee which would put together a proposal to be considered by the Common Council, the governing body of the city of New York at the time. Hamilton was approached and agreed to be part of the committee. He wanted the city to have clean drinking water.

As usual, Burr had another agenda. The Manhattan Company would also be a bank for the Republicans. In those days, banks were divided according to parties and the Federalists already had the Bank of New York which Hamilton had created. In any case, the bill for the creation of the Manhattan Water Company passed and a bank was created. In reality, the water system which was envisioned did not deliver fresh water to the city and many of the people who used it contracted yellow fever. The next year, Burr lost his seat in the Assembly and was forced to regroup.

In a twist of fate, the two adversaries, Hamilton and Burr, were to come together again and this time, they were on the same side of an issue. The issue concerned a murder trial in which Burr had a vested interest. It seemed that a young woman had been found floating in one of the wells of the Manhattan Water Company and Burr could not afford to have a scandal no less a murder associated with his scheme. So he took on the defendant, a man named Levi Weeks, and hired Hamilton to be his second chair. Amazing how circumstances can lead people to work together. Hamilton also had an interest in this trial since he was a director of the Manhattan Company. In any case, the evidence against Weeks proved to be circumstantial and Burr and Hamilton convinced the jury that Weeks was innocent and that someone else had committed the crime. Once the trial was over, Burr and Hamilton went back to be on opposite sides of the fence. Hamilton went up against Burr in several cases.

Both lawyers were overextended financially and both sank into debt.

Meanwhile Washington had died in 1799. As you remember from the earlier chapters, the next election in 1800 proved to be one of the most contentious in American history. The discussion about this election at this point might be a little bit of overkill. However, it is important to highlight it once again because of how Aaron Burr figured into the election. So here goes.

John Adams and Thomas Jefferson were the two candidates from their respective parties. But Burr was determined to get his name in the ring. He did this by working like a madman to get New York States electors to side with the Republicans. Hamilton tried valiantly to fight against Burr's campaign but in the end, Burr managed to deliver New York, which had always gone Federalist, to the Republicans, the party of Jefferson. This frenzied battle left Hamilton and Burr at loggerheads with one another. Moreover, Burr was now in a position to make demands.

In any case, Hamilton backed Thomas Pinckney for President on the Federalist side and tried to get his man to become the candidate instead of Adams. This tactic was unsuccessful but Burr was nominated to be Vice President much to Hamilton's disappointment.  While Burr was Jefferson's running mate, in 1800, Vice Presidential candidates could amass electoral votes. In other words, Burr and Jefferson could each try to get the Presidency if they got enough votes. It seems like a weird system but it was all legal according to the Constitution. In fact, if they tied for the Presidency, the House of Representatives would choose the next president.

As we saw in an earlier chapter, this is exactly what happened. Burr and Jefferson and tied with 73 votes a piece. Hamilton was appalled at the prospect of having Burr in any kind of seat of power and wrote letters to the House speaker detailing how Burr was unfit to be the President of the United States. The House of Representatives debated the issue and Burr did nothing to stop people from believing that he would ultimately become the President. The House of Representatives finally threw their support to Jefferson. Burr should have just accepted this and lobbied enough to secure the

Vice Presidency. Instead, he went back to Albany and waited it out. After much deliberation, the House voted to elect Jefferson as President and Burr as Vice President. Hamilton's worst fears were realized.

By the election of 1804, Jefferson was ready to get rid of Burr as his Vice President. Burr left Washington and threw his hat in the ring to become the next governor of New York. Incredibly, Burr was now running on the Federalist ticket and though Hamilton tried to stop him, he was unsuccessful. Burr was being supported by the party that he had scorned.

The election ended up being between Burr and a man named Morgan Lewis. For a time, it appeared as though Burr would win the election though it was a vicious campaign. Hamilton tried to discredit Burr in a series of news articles. There were also stories emerging about Burr's various affairs. Hamilton meanwhile was disgusted by what was going on and very pessimistic about the future. When the election was held, Morgan Lewis was elected to the Governorship of New York. The Burrites, as Burr's supporters were called, were sure that Burr had lost the election because of Hamilton. They claimed that his newspaper articles had undermined Burr's reputation. Burr went down to defeat and now was in disgrace. He was finished politically but he would seal his fate at the duel with Hamilton.

It is hard for people living in the modern era to understand the issue of duels and honor. There was a gentleman's code of honor which Hamilton and others lived by. It was a way of resolving arguments. However, it was more about showing you could stand up to someone rather than following through to the actual duel in which someone usually died. After the death of his son, Hamilton was less inclined to believe in or at least follow through on a threat. As we saw in the previous chapter, Hamilton was despondent over the death of his son and had gone home to be with his family. He still harbored a lot of animosity toward his archrival Burr.

Sometime during the spring of 1804, when Burr was busy running for Governor of New York, Hamilton had dinner at the home of Judge John Tayler in Albany. At the dinner table were Tayler, a Republican working for the election of Morgan

Lewis, James Kent, a Federalist, Dr. Charles Cooper, who had married Tayler's daughter, and of course Hamilton. The discussion turned to Burr and Hamilton and Kent both expressed their misgivings to everyone else about Burr. After the dinner, Cooper wrote to his friend Andrew Brown about the dinner and quoted Hamilton as saying that Burr was a "dangerous" man and was not to be trusted. Before Cooper knew it, parts of his letter were published in *The New York Evening Post* including Hamilton's remarks about Burr. Cooper claimed that the letter had been stolen. William Coleman, who was the editor, reminded his readers that Hamilton was remaining neutral in the governor's race and ran a letter in the newspaper from Phillip Schuyler, Hamilton's father-in-law in which he asserted that Hamilton would never make a statement like the one Cooper had attributed to him. Cooper became insulted and wrote another letter to Schuyler in which he said that he had heard the conversation between Hamilton and Kent and that Hamilton had called Burr a dangerous man. Moreover, he wrote that he had been very cautious in relating what had transpired at the dinner table; in fact, according to Cooper, Hamilton had said something far more damaging about Burr. Cooper called it a "despicable opinion". The letter sent by Cooper to Schuyler appeared in *The Albany Register*, a local paper, on April 24, 1804.

Burr read the letters and became enraged. He knew that Hamilton had been trying to discredit Burr for years and that during and after the presidential race of 1800, Hamilton had described him in such terms as profligate, corrupt, and lacking principles and had accused Burr of trying to take the Presidency away from Jefferson by cheating. Hamilton denied everything.  Before the election of 1800, Burr could not have gone after Hamilton because Hamilton was too much in favor in the administrations of Washington and Adams. But now, it was open season and Hamilton had just gone after his reputation. Burr's honor was at stake here.  What remains a mystery to this day, is what Cooper meant when he said that Hamilton had an "even more despicable opinion" of Burr. Burr was not a nice guy and had been involved in scandals, had been accused of cheating, and of breaking up marriages and getting his mistresses pregnant. In fact, Burr had already been slandered. In the final analysis, Cooper's letter was the excuse Burr needed to go after Hamilton.

Burr needed to act. He summoned his friend William Van Ness to his home and gave him a letter he had drafted to deliver to Hamilton. Van Ness went to Hamilton's office with the letter which demanded an explanation of what Hamilton meant by something "despicable". Hamilton received the letter and knew that he was going to be engaged in what gentlemen called "an affair of honor".

As we have followed Hamilton's life from his early days on Nevis to the day when he got the letter from Burr, Hamilton was always ready to defend his honor. He had at six different times been involved in events which might have resulted in a duel but each time, the duel had been averted. Now, there was the possibility of actually being a principal in this ritual.

Hamilton and Burr had had a long and contentious relationship with one another. Yet Hamilton knew that Burr was finished politically and he probably thought that Burr was ready to commit murder. In any case, when Hamilton received the letter from Burr on June 18, he could have stopped the whole affair by writing back that he regretted what he had said and maybe that would have been the end of it. But Hamilton, who as we have seen, had a fiery temper and often stood up for himself, did not back down. Instead, he told Van Ness, he would get back to Burr and on June 20, he wrote back to Burr that Burr's charges were too general and that he wanted a more detailed analysis of why Burr had dwelled on the word "despicable" and why Burr was so enraged. Hamilton was clearly pretty inflexible here. It was nitpicking to the extreme and Hamilton seemed to be just goading Burr into some kind of negative response. Burr who was accusing Hamilton on what he had heard third hand had taken place at a dinner party, was just as stubborn and intransigent. What a pair!

Burr responded the next day and accused Hamilton of patronizing him and using language that slandered his honor. He wanted Hamilton to retract his statement and apologize. Obviously, the war of words was escalating. Neither man would back down. Hamilton refused to retract his statements and wrote an even nastier letter to Burr in which it was clear there was no turning back. The letters continued back and forth with people like Van Ness and a man named Nathaniel Pendleton trying to resolve the argument. At one point, Burr wrote to Hamilton that he wanted him to retract any statements that he had made that were in any way derogatory. This was an impossible demand and Burr continued to escalate his demands until there was no recourse except to have a duel.

On June 27, Van Ness delivered a formal request for a duel to Pendleton and wrote that any further correspondence between the two men would have to be done through their seconds, in this case, Pendleton for Hamilton and Van Ness for Burr. After Hamilton agreed to the duel, he did not tell his wife Eliza about it. He was also very conflicted about going through with it. He had already senselessly lost a son to a duel and now was opposed at least in principle to a duel. Yet he also felt compelled to defend his honor and his reputation. Again, most of us would find it hard to believe that someone would risk his life just for his honor.

The solution to Hamilton's dilemma lay in the same strategy he had suggested to his son Phillip. He would purposely miss his opponent. He told Pendleton about his plan. Pendleton was horrified at this strategy and told Hamilton not to proceed in this manner. But Hamilton refused to reconsider. He had decided on a course and that was that. Some people who have studied Hamilton's life have suggested that Hamilton actually wanted Burr to kill him because Hamilton was very depressed about his career and his personal losses. Burr would therefore be doing him a favor if he killed him. Hamilton also might have believed that Burr really did not want to kill him because Burr, he reasoned could only lose by murdering him. In this, Hamilton was right. Burr would be finished politically if he killed Hamilton. But Burr could also be so enraged that he would kill even if it meant the end of his career. In contrast to Hamilton, Burr prepared for the duel by engaging in target practice. Burr was an expert marksman and had killed men before during the Revolutionary War.

The date for the duel was set for July 11. The place was a dueling ground in Weehawken, New Jersey. Dueling was actually illegal in both New

York and New Jersey but New York was much stricter in enforcing dueling laws than New Jersey so people from New York would row across the Hudson to settle their scores.

The two men and those who knew about the situation kept the whole thing secret. In fact, the week before the duel, Hamilton and Burr attended a meeting of the Society of Cincinnati, which was made up of a group of retired army officers from the Revolutionary War. Hamilton was the President of the Society and could not skip the meeting. He attended it in New York as did Burr and legend has it that Hamilton got up and sang a song at the meeting while Burr looked on.

Hamilton also continued with his duties as a father and husband. At the Grange, Eliza and

Alexander had begun to entertain and have elaborate parties. Hamilton no doubt felt guilty about concealing what was about to happen from his wife and children. He spent the last weeks of his life arranging his affairs and writing letters to his wife. Hamilton knew he had no money to leave Eliza but thought that between her inheritance from her father and the Grange, things would be okay for the family. Instead, Hamilton left his family in debt.

After spending time a leisurely Sunday with his family, Hamilton went down to Lower Manhattan to draft his will on July 9. Until the end, Hamilton acted as though he would survive. At one point, on July 10, he ran into a friend and client, Dirck Ten Broeck, and discussed a legal opinion that Hamilton still needed to write.

Hamilton assured his friend that he would take care of it the next day.

On the evening before the duel, Pendleton stopped by with the hope of dissuading Hamilton from his plan to give up his first shot. Hamilton refused to listen and said that he was going to fire into the air. Hamilton spent the last hours of his life at his townhouse in Lower Manhattan doing what he did best – writing. He wrote a beautiful letter to Eliza and composed a hymn for her as well.  He gave instructions that the letter and hymn were not to be delivered to her at the Grange unless he died.  Hamilton spent his last hours with his son John at the Hamilton townhouse and told John that he would be going up to the Grange in the morning so he would not worry about Hamilton when he got up in the morning and did not find him. In the morning, Hamilton got up early and went to the docks in Manhattan. Four oarsmen rowed him across the Hudson. He was accompanied by his second, Pendleton, and his family doctor, Dr. Hosack. Hamilton was dressed in his uniform and boots.

Burr's last days were spent alone. On the evening before the duel, he wrote a set of instructions about what to do with his slaves. He also wrote to his daughter Theodosia and told her to burn all of his letters and other documents which he feared would incriminate him. Burr dressed very simply and arrived first with Van Ness at Weehawken where he went to a rocky ledge which faced a stretch of Manhattan that was sparsely populated. Hamilton and his second soon joined them; they left the doctor in the boat nearby.

At 7:00 a.m., the two men stood ten paces apart ready to commence their duel. Pendleton and Van Ness drew lots (which was kind of like rolling dice) to determine where the two duelists would stand and who would be the first to fire. Pendleton won and Hamilton, weirdly enough, decided to take the northern spot which faced the sun. Burr had the advantage because he did not have the sun in his eyes. Hamilton had brought the pistols with him that were owned by John Church. These were the same pistols that Church had lent to his son Phillip.

Hamilton and Burr assumed the positions of duelists which in accepted dueling practice meant that each man would stand in profile or sideways to make it harder for the opponent to hit the other person.  Pendleton asked if the men were ready and when they both said yes, Pendleton said "Present" and the two men raised their pistols.  Two shots were fired at the same time. Burr's got there first; he hit Hamilton in the stomach right above his hip. Hamilton knew it was a fatal wound and exclaimed that he was "a dead man". Hamilton's bullet had gone above Burr's head and landed in a tree. Van Ness insisted that Hamilton had fired first. Burr told Van Ness that he had stumbled on a rock and that he had waited to fire back because the smoke from Hamilton's gun was blocking his vision.  When Pendleton went back the next day to investigate the site of the dule, he found that Hamilton's bullet was about four feet to the side of his opponent. In other words, it was never anywhere near Burr and indeed, Hamilton had done as he had planned and missed deliberately.

Once Hamilton was hit, Pendleton ran for the doctor. Hamilton was loaded into the boat where he became unconscious. Hamilton briefly regained consciousness and told Pendleton that he never intended to fire at Burr. Hamilton was carried to the house of William Bayard who lived in what is now Greenwich Village. Word of the duel spread quickly and most people reacted with horror. Eliza and the children were summoned from the Grange but at first told that Hamilton was suffering from some illness. Eliza was in great despair and she stayed with Hamilton throughout the night and into the next day. But Hamilton did not survive and died.

After Hamilton died, there was an enormous funeral in New York. Flags flew at half-staff and church bells rang in Hamilton's honor. The funeral was held in Trinity Church. Governor Morris delivered the eulogy. Hamilton died on July 11, 1804. He was forty-nine years old.

What a tragedy! Hamilton surely had a lot more to give to the country. He had certainly contributed so much to making the United States what it is today. We will end this book by briefly looking at what happened after Hamilton died.

# Epilogue

Though this book is about Alexander Hamilton, it is also about the people who surrounded him and had an influence on his life. One of the most important people in his life was his wife Eliza. Eliza lived for fifty years after Hamilton was killed at the duel in Weehawken, New Jersey.

It was Eliza who kept Hamilton's legacy alive throughout those years. We have already seen how she stood by Hamilton throughout his career. Despite the scandals and ups and downs of his life, she never wavered in her support of him. This was very admirable.

After Hamilton died, Eliza had to raise her seven children by herself. She was in debt since Hamilton had not left her much money and nor had her father. Yet she carried on and survived.

In the manner of the day, she was always dressed in black shawls and a voluminous black dress. She always wore a white frilly cap and starched ruffle both of which were a throwback to the early days of the United States. She indeed was the oldest surviving Revolutionary War widow of note.

Eliza moved to Washington D.C. and lived in a modest house on H Street. She was very religious and clung to her beliefs despite having endured such terrible tragedies as the death of her husband at early age and of her son Phillip. She continued to entertain visitors throughout her life and told them of Hamilton's exploits. She apparently always defended his honor and his legacy. She also kept many pieces from her marriage which were a tribute to Hamilton.

There was a painting of George Washington which was painted by Gilbert Stuart and next to the painting was the wine cooler that Washington sent to Eliza and Alexander during the height of the scandal with Maria Reynolds. There were also letters and other items from Hamilton's life which she treasured.

Eliza was very determined to make sure that Hamilton's reputation as a statesman and soldier remained intact. Just because Hamilton died, the slander against it did not really stop. In fact, Jefferson, Adams, and others continued to write nasty things about Hamilton and make sure that these juicy items were published and got wide circulation. Eliza decided that she would not let these horrible things stand in her way. She hired thirty people to assist her in going through his letters and other writings. Since Hamilton was a prolific writer, there was much to go through. Interestingly enough, she destroyed her own correspondence so we have very little that remains which would give us deeper insight into what made her tick.

Anyway, after going through his papers, Eliza decided to publish a biography of Hamilton that would be authorized and would secure his place in history. A very admirable thing for a widow to do. Not everyone would take on such a task. Most of the biographers Eliza approached turned her down. The gigantic book was finally taken on by her son John Church Hamilton who got together a seven volume book of Hamilton's life and his accomplishments. Eliza Hamilton died on November 9, 1854 before the biography was done. After Eliza died, her children, especially her son John and her daughter Eliza (named for her mother), kept the legacy alive and felt that it was extremely important to see that justice was done to the great man that was Alexander Hamilton.

As this book has shown, Hamilton was a great man and did leave a lasting imprint on the United States of America in numerous ways. He was so versatile in what he did considering where he came from. As an impoverished young man in the West Indies, he nevertheless was motivated enough to educate himself. Whether it was the set of books that his mother Rachel left to him which opened up new worlds to him or the education as a bookkeeper and manager for Beekman and Cruger, Hamilton never passed up an opportunity to acquire knowledge. He also was gifted with words and his piece about the hurricane on St. Croix that ultimately got him off the island was just the beginning of a long career in which he used his gift to influence the evolution of America from being just a bunch of colonists who wanted their freedom to a world powerhouse.

When he took a cause on, he truly gave his heart and soul to it. As a Revolutionary War soldier, he led his men into battle and took some high profile risks which helped the cause. While he might have chafed at being at the beck and call of Washington, he did serve him well and it is hard to imagine Washington being successful without Hamilton's help. Even though they had a falling out, Washington continued to cherish their friendship and believed in Hamilton's brainpower and ability to wordsmith Washington's ideas.

This book looked at Hamilton's accomplishments while he was involved in the young government of the United States. A currency system we all use today; a service which evolved into our present day Coast Guard; judicial review, an important part of our legal system; the foundation of America's economic system with the central bank; the implementation of an Executive Branch of the government; and a strong advocate of the Constitution on which the United States government is based. He also was instrumental in pushing for the freedom for the thousands of slaves who were living in the country. Finally,

Hamilton supported the idea of making the United States a major player in the world economy by developing manufacturing in this country. His legacy can be thought of as the foundation of entrepreneurship in the United States which enabled inventors and innovators to create amazing machines and develop great ideas. Just for starters, in the early days of the United States, there was Thomas Edison who invented the lightbulb and Alexander Graham Bell who is credited with inventing the mechanism which became the modern telephone. In our own day, the Internet and the computer are two inventions that changed the world.

As we have seen, there was also a dark side to Hamilton. Though he was a great statesman, writer and thinker, he was also a temperamental person. He was devoted to his family but chased after women among them Maria Reynolds, who almost ruined his career. Hamilton also adhered to a gentleman's code of honor which cost his son his life and also led to Hamilton's demise. Like many of great founding fathers, Hamilton had flaws which influenced his behavior.

One can only imagine what Hamilton would have accomplished had he lived. This book should entice you to explore more about his life and times. New York City is a great place to start for learning about Hamilton since there are so many sites which are connected to his life. There is a list of books I used to write this book and also some websites and other sources which you might find interesting. Hamilton will continue to engage people because he was such a fascinating and complex man. His legacy will live on.

# Selected Bibliography and Other Sources

## Books

Chernow, Ron, *Alexander Hamilton*, New York: Penguin Books, 2004.

Ferling, John, *Jefferson and Hamilton: The Rivalry that Forged a Nation*, New York: Bloomsbury Press, 2013.

Fritz, Jean, *Alexander Hamilton: The Outsider*, New York: The Penguin Group, 2011.

Knott, Stephen F. and Tony Williams, *Washington and Hamilton: The Alliance that Forged America,* Naperville, Illinois: Sourcebooks Inc., 2015.

Sedgewick, John, *War of Two: Alexander Hamilton, Aaron Burr and the Duel that Stunned the Nation*, New York: Berkley Books, 2015.

## Websites and Places of Interest

The Alexander Hamilton Awareness Society, www. The-Aha-Society.org

Hamiltonlives.com

The Hamilton Grange, National Park Service Monument, St. Nicholas Park at 141st Street, New York, New York

Morris Jumel Mansion, located in Upper Manhattan, New York, New York

Trinity Church, located in Lower Manhattan, New York, New York

Made in the USA
Columbia, SC
07 July 2020

13456586R00124